AWAKENED

Contents

Preface

When I was mature enough to contemplate the questions of "Who am I?" and "Why am I here?," they occupied my mind constantly, much like many others. From a young age, I embarked on a journey to uncover my identity, repeatedly reinventing myself until I finally felt I understood who I perceived I was. Despite the various versions of myself I encountered along the way, I never settled on just one perception.

My upbringing was not particularly religious, yet at the age of eight, I began reading the King James version of the Holy Bible on my own. Even though I struggled to grasp the content and meaning of many words at such a young age, I managed to read through the entire Bible in a matter of months. I familiarized myself with the books of the New Testament and recognized that there were different versions of the Bible beyond it. That same year, I joined a local Pentecostal Church, marking the start of my lifelong fascination with belief systems.

As my interest in ideologies, philosophy, and psychology deepened, I came to understand that my worldview was limited by my own perceptions. This realization fueled my curiosity, leading me to explore a multitude of ideologies in search of a broader perspective. In my early 30s, I delved into the teachings of Buddhism and experienced a profound shift in my understanding of reality. The concepts I encountered resonated with me in a way unlike anything I had previously encountered, including my familiarity with Christianity. The more I immersed myself in Buddhist philosophy, the clearer it became that my previous understanding of reality had been confined to a narrow perspective. It was as if I had been living in a self-created cave of perception, only venturing beyond its confines when I embraced the teachings of Buddhism.

I delved into books, sought guidance from those wiser than me, and reflected deeply on my experiences in an attempt to grasp the essence of my being. This pursuit was not just about understanding my external attributes or roles I played in society, but it was an exploration of my innermost thoughts, feelings, and desires. I questioned my beliefs, values, and motivations, trying to unravel the intricacies of my consciousness.

Each phase of my life brought forth a new perspective, a new facet of my personality that I hadn't acknowledged before. I found myself oscillating between extroversion and introversion, between confidence and self-doubt, between ambition and contentment. It was a constant cycle of self-discovery, where I would shed old layers of myself only to uncover new ones lying beneath the surface.

But despite my efforts, I realized that the more I searched for a definitive answer to the question of my identity, the more elusive it became. I began to understand that perhaps there was no singular "true" version of myself, but rather a continuous evolution of different aspects that made up the complex tapestry of who I am. Just as a kaleidoscope shifts and transforms with each turn, so too did my sense of self morph and reshape over time.

With this realization, I embraced the idea that my identity was not fixed or static, but rather fluid and adaptable. I allowed myself the freedom to explore various facets of my personality without feeling the need to confine myself to a rigid definition. This newfound perspective offered me a sense of liberation, a release from the self-imposed pressure to have everything figured out.

I came to understand that the journey of self-discovery is not about arriving at a final destination, but rather about embracing the continual process of growth and transformation. It was about learning to appreciate the complexities and contradictions within myself, accepting them as integral parts of the intricate mosaic that made me unique.

As I navigated through the twists and turns of life, I realized that my quest for self-discovery was not just about understanding who I was, but also about uncovering the deeper purpose behind my existence. I continued to ponder the question of "Why am I here?" with a sense of curiosity and awe, recognizing that there was a larger narrative at play beyond my identity.

I delved deeply into theology, ideologies, philosophy, spirituality, and science, seeking to unravel the mysteries of my place in the universe. I explored the interconnectedness of all living beings, the cosmic patterns that governed existence, and the profound beauty of the human experience. In my quest for meaning, I found solace in the realization that my existence was not accidental or arbitrary, but rather a part of a grand tapestry of creation. Just like viewing a true tapestry, the millions of colorful threads weaving around each other, when viewed individually, revealed just the threads, but when viewed as a whole, the true picture reveals itself in amazing detail.

As I contemplated my purpose in the vast expanse of existence, I realized that it was not just about achieving personal success or fulfilling societal expectations. It was about making a positive impact on the world around me, contributing my unique gifts and talents to the greater good. I began to realize that my perception was just a cave, and there was a whole new world on the other side of the cave wall. I saw that my purpose was intertwined with the well-being of others, that my actions had the power to ripple outwards and create a chain reaction of positivity and transformation.

With this newfound clarity, I embarked on a journey of service and compassion, seeking to make a difference in the lives of those around me. Starting in high school, I joined the most prestigious club in school, the Key Club. I learned the value of civic service, and I volunteered at local community organizations, offered a helping hand to those in need, and strived to spread kindness and empathy wherever I went. I discovered a profound sense of fulfillment in connecting with others, in sharing in their joys and sorrows, and being a source of support and love.

Through my acts of kindness and generosity, I began to see the impact of my actions reverberating throughout my world. I witnessed how a simple smile could brighten someone's day, how a listening ear could provide solace in times of distress, how a small gesture of kindness could ignite a spark of hope in others when their world was filled with darkness. I understood that my purpose was not just about what I could gain for myself, but about what I could give to others.

As I immersed myself in a life of service and compassion, I found that my sense of self expanded beyond the confines of my individual identity. I saw myself as a thread in the intricate tapestry of humanity, woven together with countless others in a symphony of interconnectedness and unity. I realized that my purpose was not just about my personal fulfillment, but about contributing to the greater good of all beings.

In this realization, I discovered a profound sense of peace and harmony within myself. I no longer felt the need to search for a static definition of who I was, for I understood that my identity was a fluid and ever-evolving expression of the divine spark within me. I embraced the journey of self-discovery as a sacred pilgrimage, a continuous exploration of my inner landscape and the vast expanse of the cosmos.

With each passing day, I allowed myself to be guided by the whispers of the universe, to follow the path of love and compassion that led me towards a deeper understanding of my purpose in this world. I surrendered to the flow of life, trusting in the wisdom of the universe to guide me towards my highest truth. And in that surrender, I found a sense of peace and fulfillment that transcended any external definition of success or achievement.

As I look back on the journey that brought me to this moment, I am filled with gratitude for all the twists and turns, the challenges and triumphs, the moments of doubt and moments of clarity, and I cherish the suffering that having a clouded vision of my perceived self has caused me. I see now that every step along the way was a stepping stone towards a greater understanding of myself and my place in the world. And as I continue to walk this path of self-discovery, I do so with an open heart and a trusting spirit, knowing that the universe is guiding me towards a destiny that is intricately woven into the fabric of creation.

And so, I embrace the unknown with a sense of wonder and curiosity, knowing that each new day brings with it the opportunity for growth and transformation. I embrace the ever-changing landscape of my identity, allowing myself to evolve and adapt with grace and humility. And I embrace my purpose with a deep sense of commitment and dedication, knowing that my actions have the power to shape the world in profound and meaningful ways.

I no longer desire to have the answers to "Who I am or Why am I here?". I realize that the questions of "Who am I?" and "Why am I here?" may never have a definitive answer, for they are not meant to be solved like a mathematical equation or a puzzle with a single solution. Rather, their meanings come from the life I live, and all that I experience, and I embody them with a sense of joy and wonder. And so, I continue on my journey of self-discovery with a heart full of gratitude and a spirit filled with hope, knowing that the adventure of becoming truly myself is a life-long pursuit worth every moment. Becoming awakened and realizing the illusion of the self is not going to happen by reading words on a page and listening to someone tell you how they are focusing their efforts. Each one of us has our own path and each path has many forks and twists. The ultimate purpose of this message is to illustrate that becoming awakened is possible regardless of where others are on their path. It is the acknowledgment that what lies inside your cave is not all there is to defining who you perceive your identity to be.

While I do not seek to impose the belief that Buddhism is the ultimate path to self-discovery and self-identification, it undeniably played a pivotal role in guiding me towards a deeper understanding of my own identity. The journey towards enlightenment and self-awareness is fraught with psychological challenges, as I discovered through my own experiences. In sharing my struggles and revelations, my aim is to shed light on a facet of human consciousness that often eludes comprehension without firsthand exploration. For many, this journey involves navigating a complex interplay of thoughts and beliefs that will challenge the entirety of the belief systems that make up our identity.

Having spent years exploring the depths of my psyche, I hope to offer guidance to others on a similar quest for enlightenment. By articulating the insights that have shaped my perspective, I seek to accelerate the process of self-realization for those who may be embarking on a similar journey. This narrative serves as a tangible reflection of the internal odyssey I have undertaken. It is not about persuading others to adopt my way of thinking or elevating my journey above anyone else's. Instead, it aims to provoke a shift in perception, inviting readers to contemplate their true nature and challenge their existing beliefs and realities. The content elucidates a poignant invitation for individuals to embark on a journey of self-exploration and introspection. It serves as a catalyst, urging them to delve into the profound recesses of their consciousness. The intention is to foster a greater comprehension of one's true essence while encouraging a departure from the confines of conventional self-perception and identity. This call to delve deeper into the echelons of the self stands as an opportunity for personal growth and enlightenment. By venturing into the uncharted territories of their own being, individuals may unravel hidden truths, confront inner conflicts, and ultimately, emerge with a renewed sense of self-awareness and authenticity.

What I am sharing is more relevant now than ever.

In this pivotal juncture of history, we find ourselves immersed in a profound state of oblivion, so deep that we have not only forgotten, but we have even lost awareness of the vast expanse of our forgetfulness. It is within this abyss of unknowing that the enigmatic force of Maya thrives— a potent blend of creation, illusion, and a love so ancient and boundless that it transcends all earthly constraints.

Attempting to articulate this profound truth poses a formidable challenge for the essence of human consciousness that any journey taken to enlighten oneself encapsulates. True understanding cannot be captured solely through the finite realm of written words. To truly grasp the depth of my message, one must strive to adopt and implement the concepts being presented. What you are reading here is but a mere reflection, a faint echo of the turbulent inner odyssey that has unfolded within me—a journey that seeks not to impose my beliefs or elevate my experiences above yours, but rather to provoke a seismic shift in the very fabric of your thoughts, beliefs, perceptions, and the very paradigm that defines your understanding of reality.

Wading through the murky waters of uncertainty and doubt, strive to strip bare of all pretense and falsehoods that once cloaked the essence of your perception of the reality that you created for yourself. Each step forward is a battle cry, a brazen defiance against the shackles of complacency that have long held the human identity of self captive. In this crucible of self-discovery, we are both the alchemist and the crucible itself, transforming leaden despair into the golden light of newfound wisdom.

This is not mere information to be passively absorbed; it is a clarion call to self-action—a relentless summons for you to delve deep within your own being, to unravel the enigma of your authentic self, and to confront the illusions that shroud your true essence. Now, more than ever, this revelation is of paramount importance, for the grip of forgetfulness tightens its hold on our collective consciousness, blurring the boundaries between reality and illusion, truth and deception.

Step lively and be a prophetic witness to the death of an illusion and the birth of the true you.

AWAKENED

The Quest for Self-Identity: Embarking on a Journey of "The Self"

Humanity is at a time in history where it has formed self-identities based on what is perceived to be reality, which the egoic construct has fueled. The act of allowing the ego to forge the self-concept has cast us into a time in which we have not only forgotten who we are, but we have forgotten what we have forgotten.

"Withdraw into yourself and look. And if you do not find yourself beautiful yet, act as does the creator of a statue that is to be made beautiful: he cuts away here, he smooths there, he makes this line lighter, this other purer, until a lovely face has grown upon his work. So, do you also:

cut away all that is excessive, straighten all that is crooked, bring light to all that is overcast, labor to make all one glow of beauty and never cease chiseling your statue, until there shall shine out on you from it the godlike splendor of virtue, until you shall see the perfect goodness surely established in the stainless shrine." Plotinus.

THE BEGINNING OF THE ODYSSEY

Let us take our first steps together as we begin an odyssey, a quest for enlightenment, defined as "the state of being free from ignorance and false beliefs." In other words, it's about seeing things as they are and understanding the truth about life and your reason for existence. The quest for enlightenment can be a lifelong journey, but there are certain things you can do to speed up the process, such as seeking wisdom and guidance from others who have journeyed through the trials and tribulations to become awakened.

To truly understand the journey undertaken to comprehend one's own identity, an initial delving into the core principles of both Psychology and religion is vital and was conducted. This exploration necessitated a comprehensive analysis and a comparative examination of how these two fields are interlaced to create a holistic understanding of the self.

By scrutinizing their intersections and divergences, the nuanced ways in which psychological theories and religious beliefs converge were uncovered, offering insights into the essence of who we are. This integrative approach allowed for a richer perspective, illuminating the influences that shape perceptions of selfhood and identity. Through this rigorous inquiry, the complexities of existence were illuminated, revealing how the interplay between mind and spirit informs the understanding of identity. Ultimately, this exploration became a vital cornerstone in the pursuit of self-awareness and personal growth.

In this dance of inquiry, the recognition began to emerge that psychology, with its emphasis on empirical evidence and the subconscious, could often be perceived as clashing with the ethereal nature of religious experiences which spoke to the soul's yearning for connection and purpose. This intrigue was prompted by this dissonance, leading to further questions: How could the measured, often clinical observations of psychology be reconciled with the life-affirming, transcendent narratives found in spiritual traditions? Were they truly at odds, or could a deeper communion be discerned upon closer examination?

As this interplay was explored, the concept of the 'self' was found to be not merely an isolated entity, but rather a dynamic construct influenced by the broader narratives of community, faith, and culture. It was realized that identity is not static, but fluid and continuously evolving, a realization that was both liberating and daunting. The conventional understanding of individualism that pervades contemporary society was challenged, inviting a paradigm to shift in which the interconnectedness of all life forms could redefine the perception of the self.

The works of Carl Rogers were encountered, whose humanistic approach emphasized the importance of self-actualization and the inherent possibility for growth within every individual. His ideas deeply resonated with me, as they aligned with many spiritual teachings that advocate for the awakening of one's true potential. A bridge between the psychological and the spiritual was established here, serving as a testament to the shared goal of both realms: the pursuit of authenticity and wholeness.

Through this lens, the struggles inherent in the quest for identity began to be viewed from a new dimension, with challenges being transformed into opportunities for self-discovery.

Various cultural perspectives on identity were explored, revealing how different societies and their religious practices shape the individual's place within the cosmos. Indigenous philosophies celebrated the interconnectedness of all beings, while Eastern religions emphasized the illusion of the self. The diverse ways in which humanity's existence has been articulated were striking. Understanding was enriched by these encounters, and a sense of humility was fostered; my own narrative was recognized as just one thread in an intricate weave of human experience.

As insights were pieced together, a compelling narrative was shaped, suggesting that the exploration of self is not a solitary endeavor but rather a communal tapestry woven from shared stories, struggles, and triumphs. The more I learned, the clearer my understanding became that embracing multifaceted identities requires not only introspection but also an openness to the wisdom that is imparted by others.

Through this collective engagement, the complexities of identity can begin to be navigated with compassion and clarity. This realization was marked as a pivotal moment in the journey—a commitment was made not only to seek one's own truth but also to honor the truths of others. It is recognized that within each unique story lies a reflection of shared humanity. This delicate balance between the self and the collective was maintained as the exploration continued further along the path toward a deeper understanding of identity in all its richness and diversity.

WESTERN PSYCHOLOGY

What Is Self-Concept in Psychology?

When individuals first meet, they often initiate conversation by sharing details about themselves, such as stating, "I'm a student," "I'm a doctor," or "I'm a hiker." These statements play a significant role in shaping our self-concept, which refers to how we perceive ourselves. In the realm of psychology, self-concept delves into the distinction between our actual identity and our ideal or envisioned self. Our self-concept influences our emotions, body image, and overall sense of identity. Renowned humanistic psychologist Carl Rogers posited that the fundamental drive of human beings is the inclination towards self-actualization, which involves realizing one's full potential and authentic self. Our self-concept, therefore, plays a crucial role in shaping our mindset, behavior, and aspirations as we navigate through life.

As we embark on our life journeys, the significance of our self-concept becomes increasingly apparent. How we define ourselves, whether as a student, a doctor, a parent, or an artist, forms the foundation of our identity. It is within this framework that we carve out our path towards self-actualization, a concept so eloquently put forth by Carl Rogers. Self-actualization beckons us to embrace our true essence and to strive for the highest version of ourselves. This pursuit is not merely about achievements or accolades; it is about aligning our actions with our innermost values and aspirations. Our self-concept acts as a compass, guiding us through the complexities of life, nudging us towards growth and authenticity. As we navigate the winds of change and the tides of experience, our self-concept remains a steadfast companion, reminding us of who we are and who we aspire to be.

Rogers champions the notion that actualizing oneself is contingent upon the harmonization of one's ideal self with one's self-image. The self-concept, a trinity comprised of self-image, ideal-self, and self-worth, forms the bedrock of this transformative journey. Self-image mirrors how a person views themselves physically and mentally, while the ideal self embodies the individual they aspire to evolve into. On the flip side, self-worth, or self-esteem, derives its sustenance from societal interactions and external evaluations.

As the protagonist embarks on the arduous path of self-discovery, they realize that aligning these three components of the self-concept is paramount to unlocking their full potential. It becomes evident that self-image acts as a looking glass, reflecting not only their physical attributes but also their inner thoughts and beliefs. The ideal self serves as a beacon, guiding them towards growth and actualization, pushing the boundaries of what they believe is possible.

Yet, it is self-worth that often proves to be the most challenging aspect to balance. The protagonist grapples with the external standards imposed by society, the expectations of others weighing heavily on their shoulders. It is through introspection and inner strength that they begin to dismantle these external influences and forge a self-worth that is independent and resilient.

In this self-realization journey, the protagonist learns that true fulfill-ment comes from within, from the alignment of self-image, ideal-self, and self-worth. As they continue to navigate the complexities of their psyche, they gain a deeper understanding of themselves and the world around them. And in this synergy of self-concept, they find the key to unlocking their boundless potential and living a life that is authentically their own.

In essence, the realization of self, according to Rogers, pivots on the alignment of one's ideal self with one's self-image. This foundational principle is bolstered by the triad of self-image, ideal-self, and self-worth. These constituents synergize to sculpt an individual's self-concept, propelling them towards the pinnacle of self-actualization.

SELF-IMAGE IN PSYCHOLOGY

Psychologists delve into the intricacies of self-image, intrigued by its impact on our choices and interactions. Self-image encapsulates our subjective perception of ourselves in terms of appearance and identity. It encompasses the intricate tapestry of how we view ourselves - whether as attractive, humorous, skilled, self-centered, or compassionate. Distinguishing self-image from self-concept is essential. While self-image focuses on our perception of our traits and physical attributes, self-concept paints a broader picture of our overall identity - encompassing physical, mental, social, and even spiritual dimensions.

Formed and molded over time, our self-concept evolves through a dynamic process influenced by various factors. Ashton, for instance, exudes confidence in her musical prowess and stage presence, attributing her success to her exceptional talent and allure. However, as she matures and gains exposure to different viewpoints and comparisons with her peers and accomplished musicians, her self-concept undergoes scrutiny. External feedback and self-reflection gradually shape and refine her self-concept, prompting introspection and reevaluation of her abilities and public persona.

Central to the foundation of our self-concept are fundamental beliefs that we hold to be true about ourselves. These beliefs serve as guiding principles, anchoring our identity and providing a framework for self-assessment and interaction with the world. As we navigate through life's complexities, our self-concept serves as a compass, steering our actions, shaping our perceptions, and influencing our relationships.

Our self-concept is a dynamic entity, constantly evolving in response to our experiences and the feedback we receive from others. It is both a reflection of our past and a projection of our future aspirations. By understanding and nurturing our self-concept, we empower ourselves to grow, adapt, and thrive amidst life's ever-changing landscape. Embracing the complexities of our inner world allows us to better understand the complexities of the outer world, fostering empathy, resilience, and authentic connections with those around us.

KEY PRINCIPLES OF SELF CONCEPT

The amalgamation of self-esteem, self-knowledge, and the social self forms the self-concept—a dynamic interplay between one's ideal self and one's actual self. This concept evolves through feedback and social interactions, constantly adapting to new experiences. Five fundamental principles underpin the self-concept:

1. Change: Social interactions instigate changes in self-concept as individuals collect feedback and insights from various social settings. This ongoing process continually shapes and refines one's self-perception.

2. Stability: Self-concept is also influenced by the consistent and predictable patterns in social interactions. Through these encounters, individuals gain a deeper understanding of their capabilities, emotions, and individuality. Repeated interactions enhance predictability and foster a more accurate self-concept.

3. Protection: Self-concept serves as a protective mechanism during instances where discrepancies arise between the actual self and the ideal self. Such conflicts can trigger feelings of anxiety, depression, or even aggression, highlighting the crucial role of self-concept in maintaining psychological well-being.

4. Problem-solving: Self-concept adopts a holistic perspective, drawing insights from past social interactions to navigate future engagements. By leveraging previous experiences, individuals can assess and navigate new interactions more effectively, aiding in personal growth and development.

5. Improvement: Self-concept propels individuals towards self-improvement for survival and fulfillment. The interplay between the actual self and the ideal self fuels the pursuit of growth in various aspects of life, motivating individuals to strive for excellence as parents, students, friends, and beyond.

Humanistic psychologists have delved into the realms of self-esteem, self-knowledge, and self-concept, constructing theories that elucidate these constructs' influence on individual behaviors and psychological conditions.

Humanistic psychologists have provided valuable insights into the complex nature of self-esteem, self-knowledge, and self-concept. By understanding how these constructs influence individual behaviors and psychological well-being, we can better support personal growth and foster positive self-development.

THEORIES OF SELF CONCEPT

Psychological theorists universally agree that self-concept is not something we are born with but rather something we learn over time. It encompasses our overall perception of ourselves and the judgments we make about our own identity. Both biological and environmental factors play a role in shaping our self-concept, but it is primarily through social interaction that it truly begins to take form. As we grow and evolve, so too does our self-concept, although it becomes increasingly resistant to change in later years as we solidify our sense of identity. Psychologists have put forth various theories to elucidate the complexities of self-concept and its development processes. These theories seek to provide insight into how individuals come to understand and define themselves within the context of their own lives and the world around them.

One prominent theory that explores the formation of self-concept is the social identity theory, which posits that individuals derive a significant part of their self-concept from the groups they belong to. This theory underscores the importance of social categorization and comparisons in shaping how we view ourselves. Another influential theory is the self-discrepancy theory, which suggests that our self-concept is influenced by the gaps between our actual, ideal, and ought selves. These perceived disparities can lead to feelings of dissatisfaction or internal conflict, impacting our overall self-esteem and well-being.

Moreover, the self-concept is not rigid or fixed but rather dynamic and malleable. Our experiences, interactions, and life events continuously shape and reshape our self-concept throughout our lifespan. This fluidity allows for personal growth, adaptation, and the potential for self-improvement. However, it also means that our self-concept is vulnerable to external influences, such as societal norms, media representations, and the expectations of others.

Understanding the intricacies of self-concept is crucial in fostering self-awareness, self-acceptance, and personal development. By exploring the layers of our self-perception and reflecting on the factors that contribute to its formation, we can cultivate a deeper understanding of ourselves and enhance our emotional and psychological well-being. Ultimately, embracing our self-concept as a complex and evolving construct empowers us to navigate the complexities of our inner world and forge a more authentic connection with ourselves and those around us.

Numerous authors have delved into the intricacies of the Self-concept. Within the realm of Western Psychology, it encompasses a comprehensive understanding of our physical, mental, social, and spiritual dimensions. Our Self-concept evolves gradually as we assimilate new information about ourselves, drawing insights from both internal introspection and external feedback from others.

Exploring the depths of our Self-concept allows us to navigate the complex interplay between our perception of self and how the world around us perceives us. It serves as the foundation upon which we build our identity and make sense of our place in the vast tapestry of existence. As we journey through life, our Self-concept undergoes transformations, shaped by experiences that challenge our beliefs, values, and understanding of who we are. Understanding and nurturing our Self-concept is an ongoing process that requires introspection, self-awareness, and a willingness to embrace growth and change.

Abraham Maslow

Abraham Maslow, a prominent psychologist, is well-known for his theory of the hierarchy of needs. According to Maslow, individuals have a specific order of needs that must be fulfilled, progressing from basic physiological requirements to self-actualization.

In his theory, Maslow highlighted the significance of self-esteem in the journey towards self-actualization. He asserted that individuals must feel respected and valued by themselves and others to reach their full potential. This emphasis on self-esteem as a core human motivation has had a lasting impact on the field of psychology.

Maslow's theory focused on human needs and desires rather than the problematic behaviors often studied by his colleagues in psychology. He believed that all individuals aspire to maximize their potential, coining the term "self-actualization" to encapsulate this desire. According to Maslow, people must fulfill their basic needs before they can pursue self-actualization.

At the foundation of Maslow's hierarchy are physiological needs such as food, water, and shelter. Once these needs are met, individuals can progress to the next levels of safety, love and belonging, and self-esteem (which is a crucial component of self-concept). Maslow, alongside fellow humanistic psychologist Carl Rogers, shared a belief in self-actualization as the pinnacle of human growth, where individuals strive to actualize their inherent potential.

Carl Rogers

In the realm of psychology, Carl Rogers' self-concept theory holds a prominent place. According to Rogers, the self-concept is continuously molded through self-evaluation and comparison to others. This theory posits that individuals strive to maintain harmony between their self-concept and their actual experiences and behaviors. Rogers emphasized the significance of unconditional positive regard in nurturing a healthy self-concept. He believed that receiving acceptance and support without judgment from others can lead to a positive self-concept and overall well-being.

As a humanistic psychologist, Carl Rogers believed that the pursuit of self-actualization propels our personalities. He proposed that self-concept comprises three fundamental aspects: Self-Image (how we perceive ourselves), Ideal-Self (the person we aspire to be), and Self-Worth (how much value we place on ourselves). Rogers suggested that when a person's self-image and ideal image are incongruent, their self-worth is affected. Congruence occurs when one's ideal self aligns closely with one's experience, although total congruence is rare.

Michael Lewis

Psychologist Michael Lewis introduced two essential components in the development of individual self-concept: the Existential Self (realization of individual existence separate from others) and the Categorical Self (recognition of oneself as an individual entity with distinct characteristics). With age, the Categorical Self expands to include psychological traits. Both Rogers and Lewis emphasize the impact of social interaction and learning on the formation of self-concept across different developmental stages.

As children grow, their self-concept begins to take shape, influenced by various factors such as social interactions and personal experiences. Psychologist Michael Lewis identified two significant components in this process: the Existential Self and the Categorical Self. The Existential Self represents the understanding of our existence as separate individuals, while the Categorical Self involves recognizing our unique characteristics.

It is through interactions with others that children start to develop a sense of self. As they navigate different social settings and learn more about themselves, their Categorical Self expands to include psychological traits. This development is crucial in shaping their identity and how they perceive themselves in relation to the world around them.

Both Carl Rogers and Michael Lewis underscore the importance of social interaction and learning in the formation of self-concept at various stages of development. With each new experience and encounter, children continue to refine their understanding of who they are and how they fit into the intricate tapestry of human existence.

DEVELOPMENT OF THE SELF CONCEPT

Throughout one's life, social interaction and learning play a crucial role in shaping the self-concept. Psychologists emphasize that various stages of development significantly impact how individuals perceive themselves. Whether it is through interactions with family, peers, or society at large, our self-concept is constantly evolving based on our experiences and personal growth. From childhood to old age, each stage brings unique challenges and opportunities for self-reflection and self-discovery. Understanding the impact of social interactions and learning on the development of self-concept can provide valuable insights into our behavior, relationships, and overall sense of identity. By acknowledging the importance of these factors, individuals can cultivate a more authentic and confident sense of self.

As individuals move through different stages of life, the way they perceive themselves is deeply intertwined with their social interactions and learning experiences. During childhood, interactions with family members and peers shape the foundation of one's self-concept. The feedback received from loved ones and the experiences encountered gradually form the individual's understanding of themselves.

Moving into adulthood, the importance of personal growth and self-reflection becomes paramount. Through diverse experiences and continuous learning, individuals have the opportunity to deepen their understanding of themselves. Social interactions serve as a mirror through which one can assess their beliefs, values, and behaviors, further refining their self-concept.

In later stages of life, the accumulated wisdom and life experiences shape a more mature and nuanced self-concept. With a deeper sense of self-awareness, individuals can embrace their unique identity and navigate relationships with greater authenticity and confidence.

By recognizing the profound impact of social interactions and learning on the development of self-concept, individuals can embark on a journey of self-discovery and personal growth. Embracing these influences as integral parts of one's identity allows for a more resilient and grounded sense of self, enriched by the wisdom gained through each stage of life.

Early Childhood

Early Childhood Development and Self-Concept Formation

Early childhood, encompassing the period from birth to six years old, is a critical phase in a child's life characterized by significant developmental milestones that shape their self-concept. During this time, children experience rapid changes in their physical, cognitive, emotional, and social development, which play a pivotal role in the formation of their sense of self.

Birth to 2 Years Old: Building Security Through Relationships

In the initial years of life, infants rely heavily on loving and nurturing relationships with caregivers to establish a sense of security and trust in the world around them. This early attachment serves as the foundation for their self-concept, influencing how they perceive themselves and others. Through interactions with caregivers, infants begin to develop a basic awareness of self, gradually differentiating themselves from the external environment. Research has shown that the quality of these early relationships has a profound impact on children's self-esteem and self-confidence later in life. Infants who experience consistent and responsive caregiving are more likely to develop a secure attachment style, which lays the groundwork for healthy self-concept formation.

Toddler Years: Emerging Sense of Self

As children transition into the toddler years, typically between the ages of 1 and 3, they start to assert their independence and autonomy. The emergence of self-awareness marks this period, as toddlers begin to recognize themselves in mirrors and understand that they are separate individuals from their caregivers. Through exploration and play, they develop a basic understanding of "me" and "not me," forming the building blocks of their self-concept. During this stage, clear and consistent guidance from caregivers is crucial in helping children navigate their burgeoning sense of self. Positive reinforcement and encouragement can boost their self-esteem and confidence, while redirection and limit-setting help establish boundaries and shape appropriate behaviors.

Ages 3-4: Formation of Identity

Between the ages of 3 and 4, children continue to refine their self-concept and identity by exploring their likes, dislikes, and talents. They become more aware of their individual strengths and weaknesses, seeking validation and approval from others to shape their self-image. Peer interactions and social comparisons play a significant role in how children perceive themselves and their abilities at this stage. Despite gaining a more distinct sense of self, young children in this age group still rely heavily on external judgments and feedback to define their actions and behaviors. They may seek validation from parents, teachers, and peers to validate their self-worth and capabilities, indicating a continued reliance on external sources for self-definition.

Ages 5-6: Transition to Collective Identity

By the time children reach the ages of 5 to 6, many of them are exposed to formal schooling or other social environments outside their immediate family circle. This expansion of social interactions and experiences prompts the development of a collective identity, as children begin to identify with groups beyond their individual selves. In school settings, children learn to navigate group dynamics, form friendships, and participate in collaborative activities that shape their sense of belonging and social identity. They begin to understand their place within larger social contexts, recognizing the importance of cooperation, empathy, and shared values in building relationships with others.

Implications for Future Growth and Development

Early childhood is a crucial developmental stage that lays the groundwork for a child's future growth and learning. The formation of a secure self-concept during these formative years sets the stage for healthy relationships, positive self-esteem, and adaptive coping strategies later in life. Parents, caregivers, and educators play a vital role in supporting children's self-concept development through nurturing relationships, positive reinforcement, and opportunities for exploration and self-discovery. In conclusion, early childhood is a transformative period characterized by significant changes in physical, cognitive, emotional, and social development that shape children's self-concept. By understanding the stages of self-concept formation during early childhood and providing the necessary support and guidance, we can foster healthy self-esteem, resilience, and positive identity development in young children.

Middle Childhood

Middle childhood is a critical developmental stage that encompasses the ages of 7 to 11 years old. During this period, children are actively involved in seeking acceptance and integration within social groups, which greatly influences their self-perception. The interactions and dynamics within these social settings are pivotal in shaping how children view themselves and others around them. This is a crucial time when children assess and form their identities based on the feedback they receive from peers and their level of acceptance within these groups. Moreover, middle childhood is characterized by a shift in focus from merely conforming to group norms to striving for personal achievements and milestones that contribute to their self-concept. In middle childhood, children are transitioning from being highly influenced by external factors to developing a sense of autonomy and individuality. They begin to place greater emphasis on personal accomplishments and goals, which play a significant role in shaping their self-esteem and self-worth. It is during this stage that children start to define themselves based on their abilities, achievements, and unique qualities, rather than solely relying on external validation from social groups. This shift in focus marks an important milestone in their cognitive and emotional development as they navigate their social identities and strive for recognition within their peer circles. Research indicates that the experiences and relationships children cultivate during middle childhood have a lasting impact on their overall well-being and mental health. Positive social interactions and acceptance within peer groups are linked to higher levels of self-esteem, confidence, and emotional resilience. Conversely, children who experience rejection, social exclusion, or bullying during this stage may face challenges in developing a positive self-image and healthy social relationships. Therefore, it is essential for parents, educators, and caregivers to support children in building strong social skills and fostering positive relationships during this critical period of development.

Furthermore, middle childhood is a time when children begin to explore their interests, talents, and passions, which can significantly shape their future aspirations and goals. Encouraging children to participate in extracurricular activities, hobbies, and creative pursuits not only enhances their sense of identity but also fosters a sense of accomplishment and competence. By providing opportunities for children to explore and develop their skills and interests, caregivers can help them build a strong foundation for future success and well-being. As children progress through middle childhood, they also experience cognitive growth and enhanced problem-solving abilities. Their expanding social networks and interactions with peers enable them to learn important skills such as conflict resolution, negotiation, and empathy. These social skills are crucial in helping children navigate complex social situations and form meaningful relationships with others. Additionally, the cognitive development that takes place during middle childhood sets the stage for higher-level thinking, academic achievement, and independent decision-making in later stages of development.

Middle childhood is a pivotal stage of development where children are actively constructing their identities, seeking validation within social groups, and exploring their interests and abilities. This period represents a crucial juncture in their cognitive, emotional, and social development, laying the foundation for future growth and success. By supporting children in developing strong social skills, fostering positive relationships, and empowering them to pursue their passions, caregivers play a key role in promoting healthy development and well-being during middle childhood.

Adolescence

Adolescence is a critical period of development marked by significant physical changes, exploration of identity, and the quest for autonomy. This stage typically occurs between the ages of 12 and 18 and is characterized by a heightened sense of self-evaluation and personal growth.

Adolescents are constantly shaping their self-concept, which influences their behavior, relationships, and overall well-being well into adulthood. Physical growth is a prominent aspect of adolescence, with individuals experiencing rapid changes in height, weight, and hormonal fluctuations. These physical transformations can affect an adolescent's self-perception and body image. The way adolescents view themselves, their bodies, and their appearance can have lasting implications on their self-esteem and confidence.

Moreover, adolescents engage in a process of identity exploration during this period. They grapple with questions of who they are, what they believe in, and where they fit in the world. This quest for identity can lead to experimentation with different roles, interests, and ideologies as they try to establish a sense of self that aligns with their values and aspirations. Family dynamics play a crucial role in shaping adolescents' self-concept. Children who grow up in a supportive and nurturing family environment are more likely to develop a secure sense of self-worth and confidence. Conversely, those who experience neglect, abuse, or lack of emotional support may struggle with feelings of inadequacy and low self-esteem.

Psychologists emphasize the importance of self-concept in adolescence, which refers to how individuals perceive themselves in terms of their abilities, attributes, and overall worth. Discrepancies between one's self-image and ideal self can lead to internal conflicts and feelings of inadequacy.

Adolescents often compare themselves to their peers, media representations, and societal standards, which can contribute to unrealistic expectations and negative self-perceptions. In addition to family influence, peers and societal norms also play a significant role in shaping adolescents' self-concept. The desire to belong, fit in, and be accepted by others can lead to conformity and adherence to social expectations. Adolescents may struggle with maintaining a balance between asserting their individuality and seeking approval from their peers, leading to fluctuations in self-esteem and self-confidence.

During adolescence, individuals are more susceptible to external influences and societal pressures, which can impact their self-perception and self-worth. Social media, advertising, and popular culture contribute to unrealistic beauty standards, materialistic values, and unrealistic portrayals of success, which can distort adolescents' perceptions of themselves and others. Moreover, the transition from childhood to adolescence involves navigating complex social dynamics, establishing new relationships, and asserting independence from parents and caregivers.

Adolescents may face challenges in establishing their autonomy while seeking validation and support from their social circles. Balancing the need for independence with the desire for belonging can create inner conflicts and insecurities that shape their self-concept. In conclusion, adolescence is a transformative period marked by physical, cognitive, and emotional changes that influence individuals' self-concept and identity formation. Understanding the factors that contribute to a healthy self-concept, such as supportive family relationships, positive peer interactions, and realistic self-perceptions, is crucial in promoting adolescents' well-being and mental health.

By fostering a sense of self-worth, resilience, and self-acceptance, adolescents can navigate the challenges of this developmental stage with confidence and authenticity.

SELF CONCEPT EXAMPLES

Self-concept encompasses an individual's self-beliefs, which can be a mix of positive and negative attributes. Consider a college student who views themselves as intelligent, striving for academic success, yet feels inadequate in athletic endeavors and shies away from competitiveness. They may even feel envious of a sporty family member. Similarly, an adult might see themselves as a diligent worker, highly capable, and a top-notch employee, while receiving feedback from others that they neglect their relationships due to work commitments. This discrepancy between self-perception and external evaluations can create a conflict between one's ideal self and actual self-image, leading to a complex self-concept.

This internal struggle often manifests in different aspects of one's life, causing confusion and inner turmoil. The clash between what one believes about themselves, and the feedback received from others can create a sense of insecurity and self-doubt.

For the college student, excelling academically might bring a sense of accomplishment and pride. Yet, the inability to measure up in sports or social settings may trigger feelings of inadequacy and envy. The constant comparison to a more athletic family member can further fuel these negative emotions, reinforcing the belief of not being good enough in certain areas.

Similarly, the hardworking adults may pride themselves on being a dedicated employee, giving their all to their job and achieving professional success. However, the criticism about neglecting personal relationships due to work commitments can cast a shadow of doubt on their self-perception. The realization that their actions might be negatively impacting their personal life can lead to feelings of guilt and a questioning of their priorities.

Navigating these discrepancies between their ideal self and the feedback from others can be a challenging journey. It requires introspection, acceptance of flaws, and a willingness to work on aligning their self-concept with reality. Only through self-awareness and a willingness to grow can they bridge the gap between their perceived self-image and external evaluations, ultimately fostering a more balanced and authentic sense of self.

Human nature is intricately connected to the concept of the self, dictating that individuals strive to excel in their relationships, academia, and careers. The self-concept serves as a framework that navigates the interactions and conflicts between the ideal self (our envisioned best version) and the self-image (our personal perception and mental images of ourselves). When these two facets are not in sync or do not align, it can have a direct impact on an individual's self-esteem and self-worth. Humanistic psychologists delve into the study of the self-concept, examining its effects on people's lives, particularly when it leads to issues like anxiety and challenges with self-worth. The ultimate objective for individuals is to attain self-actualization, aspiring to reach their fullest potential in life. Maslow introduced the theory of the Hierarchy of Needs, a visual depiction illustrating the progression of needs that must be fulfilled before one can achieve self-actualization.

According to Carl Rogers, a harmonious fusion of the self-image and the ideal self results in a more congruent and stable self-concept. Individuals shape their self-concept at various stages of their lives, with each phase playing a crucial role in defining their self-perception. Throughout the stages of development, individuals can significantly influence the self-worth of their offspring, which refers to the perceived sense of value or worth they hold. The self-concept continuously strives to establish equilibrium by addressing challenges, processing feedback, adapting based on social interactions, and evolving for the betterment of the individual.

Self-concept is a fundamental aspect of human psychology, encompassing an individual's self-beliefs and perceptions about themselves. It can be a complex mix of positive and negative attributes that shape how individuals see themselves and navigate their interactions with the world around them. In the examples provided, we see how self-concept influences various aspects of individuals' lives, impacting their behaviors, emotions, and relationships. For instance, the college student in the example views themselves as intelligent and academically successful but feels inadequate in athletic endeavors. This discrepancy between feeling competent in one area and lacking in another can create inner turmoil and insecurity. The student's self-concept is further complicated by feelings of envy towards a more athletic family member, highlighting how external comparisons can affect one's self-perception.

Similarly, the adult in the example sees themselves as a diligent worker and a top-notch employee but receives feedback about neglecting personal relationships due to work commitments. This discordance between professional success and personal fulfillment can lead to feelings of guilt and questioning of priorities. The adult's self-concept is challenged by the need to balance work and personal life, illustrating the complexities of maintaining a cohesive self-image.

The clash between one's ideal self (the envisioned best version of oneself) and the self-image (personal perception and mental images of oneself) can create a gap that impacts self-esteem and self-worth. Humanistic psychologists explore the effects of self-concept on individuals, particularly when discrepancies lead to issues such as anxiety and challenges with self-worth. The journey towards self-actualization, as proposed by Maslow's Hierarchy of Needs, involves fulfilling basic needs before aspiring to reach one's fullest potential in life. Carl Rogers emphasized the importance of achieving congruence between the self-image and the ideal self to develop a stable and authentic self-concept. This harmonious fusion involves introspection, acceptance of flaws, and alignment of self-perception with reality. Individuals shape their self-concept through various stages of development, with each phase influencing their self-perception and self-worth.

The continuous process of addressing challenges, processing feedback, adapting to social interactions, and evolving for personal growth is essential for maintaining a balanced and authentic sense of self. Expanding on this discussion, it is important to delve deeper into the psychological theories and research related to self-concept. Understanding the factors that contribute to the formation and development of self-concept can provide valuable insights into how individuals perceive themselves and navigate their lives.

Researchers have identified several key elements that influence self-concept, including social comparisons, feedback from others, personal experiences, and cultural influences. Social comparisons play a significant role in shaping self-concept by providing reference points for evaluating one's abilities and attributes. Individuals often compare themselves to others in various domains, such as academics, relationships, and career success. These comparisons can have both positive and negative effects on self-concept, depending on whether the individual perceives themselves as superior or inferior to others in a particular area.

Feedback from others also plays a crucial role in shaping self-concept. Positive feedback that reinforces one's strengths and abilities can enhance self-esteem and self-confidence. Conversely, negative feedback or criticism can lead to feelings of inadequacy and self-doubt, contributing to a more negative self-concept. The way individuals interpret and internalize feedback from others can shape their self-perception and influence their behavior and mindset. Personal experiences, including successes, failures, challenges, and achievements, contribute to the formation of self-concept. Individuals often draw upon past experiences to construct their self-image and beliefs about themselves. Positive experiences that validate one's abilities and talents can bolster self-esteem, while negative experiences that challenge one's self-perception can create insecurities and doubts.

The accumulation of life experiences shapes how individuals see themselves and influences their self-concept over time. Cultural influences play a significant role in shaping self-concept by providing norms, values, and expectations that guide individuals' self-perception. Cultural factors such as ethnicity, religion, social class, and gender norms influence how individuals define themselves and their place in society. These cultural influences can impact the ideals and standards individuals aspire to meet, shaping their self-concept in both conscious and unconscious ways.

Psychological research on self-concept has explored various theories and models that help explain how individuals perceive themselves and maintain a cohesive self-image. One prominent theory is social comparison theory, which posits that individuals evaluate their abilities and attributes by comparing themselves to others. This comparative process influences self-evaluation and contributes to the formation of self-concept. Social comparison theory highlights the role of social interactions and external influences in shaping self-concept.

Another influential theory is self-discrepancy theory, which proposes that individuals compare their actual self (how they see themselves) to their ideal self (how they want to be) and their ought self (how they think they should be). Discrepancies between these self-guides can lead to emotional discomfort and impact self-esteem. Self-discrepancy theory emphasizes the importance of aligning one's self-concept with their internal standards and values to maintain psychological well-being. In addition to theoretical frameworks, researchers have also examined the relationship between self-concept and psychological well-being. Studies have shown that individuals with a positive self-concept tend to experience higher levels of self-esteem, self-efficacy, and life satisfaction.

A healthy self-concept is associated with greater resilience, adaptive coping strategies, and positive mental health outcomes. Conversely, individuals with a negative self-concept may struggle with low self-esteem, self-doubt, and psychological distress. Furthermore, research has demonstrated the impact of self-concept on interpersonal relationships and social interactions. Individuals with a strong and secure self-concept are more likely to form healthy and fulfilling relationships, communicate effectively, and assert their needs and boundaries. A balanced self-concept allows individuals to navigate social dynamics, resolve conflicts, and maintain positive connections with others.

In contrast, individuals with an unstable or negative self-concept may experience challenges in forming and maintaining relationships, leading to feelings of isolation and loneliness. The implications of self-concept research extend beyond individual well-being to broader societal issues such as identity formation, diversity, and inclusion.

Understanding how self-concept is shaped by cultural, social, and psychological factors can inform interventions and policies aimed at promoting positive self-perception and self-esteem among diverse populations. By addressing the underlying factors that influence self-concept, we can create supportive environments that foster self-acceptance, self-confidence, and personal growth for all individuals. In conclusion, self-concept is a multifaceted aspect of human psychology that influences how individuals perceive themselves, interact with others, and navigate the complexities of daily life. By exploring the theories, research, and implications of self-concept, we gain valuable insights into the factors that shape our self-perception and self-esteem. Understanding the role of social comparisons, feedback from others, personal experiences, and cultural influences in shaping self-concept can help individuals cultivate a healthy and balanced sense of self. Ultimately, fostering a positive self-concept is essential for promoting well-being, resilience, and positive relationships both within us and with others in our interconnected world.

THE RELATIONSHIP BETWEEN PSYCHOLOGY AND RELIGION

Psychology and religion, though seemingly distinct disciplines, share a fundamental commonality in their grappling with the elusive nature of truth and reality. Both fields necessitate an act of faith, a willingness to embrace the intangible and the mystical. Additionally, the leaders of these domains, be they psychologists or religious authorities, are tasked with the sacred duty of alleviating the suffering of their constituents.

The primary distinction lies in their respective focal points. While religion delves into the deeper questions of life's meaning and purpose, psychology attributes significance to the individual's lived experience. However, these apparent differences belie the underlying similarities that bind these two realms of human understanding. By examining the perspectives of influential figures like Sigmund Freud and William James, and applying their insights to the characters in Chaim Potok's seminal work, "The Chosen," we can uncover the profound kinship between psychology and religion.

An in-depth analysis of Freud and James' contributions to these domains will shed light on how, despite their ostensible conflicts, they can, in fact, complement each other, fostering a more holistic and well-rounded worldview. Freud's groundbreaking work, "Totem and Taboo," posited that religion emerged from primal human urges and psychological needs. He argued that the adult's desire for divine, fatherly protection was rooted in the infant's need for the father's safeguarding. This, Freud believed, was a coping mechanism to neutralize the unpredictable and often incomprehensible realities of the world. Freud's hypothetical narrative of a clan of brothers murdering and cannibalizing their father, only to later revive him through totemistic religion, echoes similar creation myths found across cultures. However, Freud's version fundamentally departs from the traditional. Unlike other creation myths that form the foundation of religious belief, Freud's narrative condemns religion as a psychological disorder, characterized by psychosis, delusion, and compulsion. This tension between religion and psychology highlights a fundamental dilemma. The empirical, scientific framework of psychology struggles to accommodate the supernatural, divine beings that are central to religious belief. As a result, many psychologists and scientists have been wary of engaging with the study of religion, unable to reconcile their rational, evidence-based approach with the authority of revelation.

Freud, despite his own religious background, remained a staunch atheist, seemingly viewing psychoanalysis as a replacement for religion. Yet, the relationship between science and religion has not always been so adversarial. During the Scientific Revolution, most scientists saw no inherent conflict between the laws of science and belief in God, with religion maintaining its primacy and science occupying a subordinate position. It was only later, as theories proposed by thinkers like Copernicus, Galileo, and Darwin challenged the traditional interpretation of Scripture, that the tension between science and religion intensified.

The development of psychology, however, has further complicated this dynamic, as both realms now grapple with the inner workings of the individual and the physical world. William James' solution to this tension claims that both science and religion are valid perspectives, but they are akin to different languages that cannot be directly compared. As David Malter aptly states, "Freud is not God in psychology," just as religions disagree on what can be known and how it can be proven. Interestingly, despite Freud's rejection of religious authority and his steadfast atheism, his understanding of the therapist's role bears a striking resemblance to the tzaddik, the revered figure in Jewish tradition described by Potok.

Both the therapist and the tzaddik are tasked with the responsibility of alleviating the suffering of their respective constituents. Like the tzaddik, the Freudian therapist must shoulder the emotional burdens of their patient, bringing their suppressed feelings to the surface and handling them with rationality.

This parallel between the responsibilities of the psychologist and the religious leader further blurs the divide between these two domains. Danny's decision to abandon his role as a tzaddik to become a psychologist, as depicted in "The Chosen," is not as radical a departure as it may seem. Reb Saunders, Danny's father and the revered tzaddik, acknowledges the psychologist's similar responsibility to the world, recognizing the common ground between these seemingly disparate vocations.

Reuven and Danny's discussions on their chosen career paths further highlight the underlying kinship between rabbis and psychologists, dispelling the illusion that science and religion are inherently at odds. The leaders of these realms both serve as intermediaries, bridging the gap between the individual and the forces that transcend the conscious mind. The psychologist acts as a conduit between the patient and their subconscious, while the tzaddik is a bridge between the people and the divine. In this light, the gulf that appears to divide science and religion reveals itself to be more superficial than it may first seem.

By delving into the perspectives of Freud and James, and applying these insights to the characters in Potok's masterpiece, we can arrive at a richer understanding of how psychology and religion, despite their apparent differences, can, in fact, complement each other, cultivating a more holistic and well-rounded worldview.

THE ROLE OF RELIGION IN SHAPING ONE'S IDENTITY

Religion serves as a fundamental component in shaping individuals' self-identity, providing a framework through which they interpret the world and understand their place within it. By adhering to a particular religious belief system, individuals often adopt the cultural heritage, traditions, and values associated with that religion, which in turn influences their sense of cultural identity.

Research has indicated a strong connection between religion and identity formation, particularly among adolescents, highlighting the role of religion in guiding individuals through processes of exploration and commitment to their identities. One key aspect through which religion influences identity is by reinforcing or challenging group identities based on factors such as gender, sexuality, race, ethnicity, and national origin.

Different religions and their developmental stages interact with individuals' identity formation processes in distinct ways, shaping their values, beliefs, and perceptions. The teachings and practices learned from religious upbringing serve as a guiding force that informs individuals' choices and behaviors, impacting their interactions with others and the broader society.

Religion also provides a profound sense of unity and purpose, aligning with Durkheim's concept of the sacred and contributing to individuals' understanding of their place within the social fabric. Research has highlighted the positive correlation between religiosity and identity formation, suggesting that individuals who engage with their religious beliefs tend to exhibit a stronger sense of commitment, purpose, and self-awareness. However, the nature and strength of this relationship may vary across different demographic groups and historical contexts, reflecting the diverse ways in which religion intersects with identity formation.

Overall, religion emerges as a significant determinant of individuals' identities, playing a pivotal role in shaping their self-concept, values, and sense of belonging. Further exploration into the intricate dynamics between religion and identity formation reveals a nuanced interplay between ideological, social, and spiritual dimensions.

Religious ideologies provide individuals with a framework through which they interpret the world and make meaning of their experiences, offering a moral compass that guides their decisions and actions. The social aspect of religion fosters community connections and shared beliefs, creating a sense of belonging and solidarity among adherents. This communal dimension of religion often serves as a key factor in shaping individuals' identities, influencing their perceptions of self and others.

Moreover, the spiritual dimension of religion offers individuals a deeper connection to transcendent realities and higher purposes, providing a sense of existential meaning and fulfillment. Through spiritual practices such as prayer, meditation, and ritual observance, individuals engage with the divine and cultivate a sense of inner peace and harmony. This spiritual engagement can profoundly impact individuals' sense of self-identity, fostering a profound sense of interconnectedness with the universe and a transcendent source of meaning. Examining the role of religion in identity formation also reveals the complex ways in which religious beliefs intersect with personal values, ethical principles, and cultural norms.

Religion often serves as a moral compass that guides individuals' ethical decision-making and shapes their attitudes towards issues such as justice, compassion, and social responsibility. By instilling moral virtues and ethical principles, religion helps individuals navigate moral dilemmas and make principled choices that reflect their core values and beliefs. Furthermore, religion exerts a significant influence on individuals' perceptions of themselves and others, shaping their attitudes towards diversity, inclusivity, and social justice. Many religions emphasize the importance of compassion, empathy, and understanding towards others, promoting values of tolerance, respect, and acceptance of diverse perspectives.

By cultivating virtues such as love, kindness, and forgiveness, religion encourages individuals to embody moral and ethical values in their interactions with others, fostering a sense of empathy and solidarity within society. In conclusion, the intricate relationship between religion and identity formation underscores the multifaceted ways in which religious beliefs, practices, and values shape individuals' self-identity and sense of purpose.

By providing a framework through which individuals interpret the world, navigate moral dilemmas, and cultivate spiritual connections, religion plays a vital role in guiding individuals through processes of self-discovery and self-realization. Through ongoing research and analysis, scholars and practitioners can continue to explore the dynamic interplay between religion and identity, deepening our understanding of how individuals' religious beliefs inform their sense of self and place within the broader social fabric.

The Distinction of the Christian Identity of Self

The Christian Identity: A Tapestry of Belief, Tradition, and the Search for Self

The Christian identity is a complex and multifaceted expression of one's relationship with the divine, the ethical principles that guide one's actions, and the sense of belonging to a global community of believers. The sources of this identity are deeply rooted in the intricate tapestry of biblical teachings, church doctrine, and the personal journey of faith that each believer undertakes.

The Bible serves as the guiding light, the very lifeblood that defines who we are, what we possess, and what we can accomplish. As we delve into its sacred pages, our minds are alert, and our hearts are open, for within these words, we are transformed, never to be the same again. The question of who the Bible says we are and how it shapes and molds us is one that deserves our utmost attention.

In this exploration, we will unpack the profound truths that lie within the Christian anthropology, delving into the intricacies of the created self, the crooked self, the resurrected self, and the transfigured self. These four distinct aspects of the Christian identity provide a comprehensive understanding of the human condition and the transformative work of God's grace.

The Created Self: Dependence and the Image of God

Christian anthropology begins with the recognition of our creaturely nature. We are brought into existence by the triune God, the maker of heaven and earth. The foundational text that has shaped the Christian imagination regarding the created self is Genesis 1, which declares that humanity is made in the image and likeness of God.

The interpretations of this image language have varied throughout history, with some associating it with the intellect or the soul, while others have viewed it as pertaining to moral agency and holy character. More recently, scholars have proposed that the image language points to humanity's role as creative and political ambassadors, or to the relational nature of human existence that mirrors the inter-trinitarian life of God.

However, the common thread in these perspectives is the acknowledgment that to be the image of God is to be defined by reference to someone else, the original source. This recognition of dependence and distinction from the Creator is crucial, for it evokes a sense of humility and attentiveness to the ways in which we are to live rightly before God as those who are not God.

Implications for Christian Identity and Ministry

These four aspects of the Christian self – the created, the crooked, the resurrected, and the transfigured – offer a comprehensive understanding of the human condition and the work of God's grace. This breadth of biblical and theological elements is essential for grasping the nuanced Christian identity.

Two implications merit further consideration. First, we must beware of a reductive Augustinian anthropology that views humanity solely through the prism of sin, neglecting the equally vital aspect of created goodness. Augustinian insights on the pervasiveness of sin and its disordering effects must be balanced with an appreciation for the beauty of God's handiwork.

Second, we must guard against reductive views of Christology that limit the redemptive change wrought in Christ to solely justifying or substitutionary aspects. The wider scope of new creation, wherein our identity is wholly bound to union with Christ, demands attention. In this union, our created and natural specificity is transfigured, becoming worthy of divine delight.

The church's mission to offer care and comfort to souls, both inside and outside its fold, requires a robust Christology that attends not only to justification but also to the transformative gift of glory. Christ assumes our plight, walks our path, and secures our glory and blessing. He delights in the distinct particularities he has created and recreated through his gracious power.

Attentiveness to the distinct, biblical sources of the Christian self is essential for appreciating the rich tapestry of Christian identity. By embracing the breadth of these anthropological elements, we can navigate the complexities of the human condition with wisdom and compassion, offering the transformative hope of the gospel to a world in need of restoration.

The Christian Identity: A Comprehensive Exploration of the Biblical Self

The Christian identity is a multifaceted and complex expression of one's relationship with the divine, the ethical principles that guide one's actions, and the sense of belonging to a global community of believers. This identity is deeply rooted in the intricate tapestry of biblical teachings, church doctrine, and the personal journey of faith that each believer undertakes.

The creation account in Genesis 1 serves as the foundational text for understanding the Christian anthropology of the created self. The declaration that humanity is made in the "image and likeness of God" (Gen 1:26-27) has been a central tenet of Christian theology, shaping the way believers understand their identity and purpose.

Throughout the history of Christian thought, scholars have proposed various interpretations of the "image of God" language. Some have linked it to the intellectual or spiritual capacities of the human person, viewing the image as a reflection of the divine mind or soul. Others have emphasized the moral and ethical dimensions, seeing the image as related to human agency and the ability to make righteous choices.

More recently, scholars have proposed alternative perspectives that broaden the understanding of the imago Dei. One such view is the idea of humanity as God's creative and political ambassadors, entrusted with the task of cultivating and governing the created order in ways that reflect the divine character and purposes. This understanding highlights the relational and participatory nature of the image, where humans are called to exercise stewardship and dominion over the earth in a manner that aligns with God's own rule and care.

Another influential perspective is the notion of the image as pointing to the relational nature of human existence, mirroring the inter-trinitarian life of the Godhead. This view emphasizes the communal and interpersonal dimensions of the imago Dei, where the ability to engage in meaningful relationships and to live in community is seen as a vital aspect of what it means to be created in the image of God.

Regardless of the specific interpretations, the common thread in these perspectives is the acknowledgment that to be the image of God is to be defined by reference to someone else, the original source. This recognition of dependence and distinction from the Creator is crucial, for it evokes a sense of humility and attentiveness to the ways in which we are to live rightly before God as those who are not God.

The Crooked Self: Sin, Iniquity, and Transgression

The biblical narrative does not present the human condition as static or unchanging. Instead, it attests to a decisive change that occurred through the fall into sin, as recounted in Genesis 3. This event, known as the "state of humanity in Adam," has profoundly altered the human condition, giving rise to the crooked self.

The Book of Numbers provides a vivid portrayal of this crooked self, particularly in the narrative of the wilderness generation. Their refusal to trust God and obey his call to enter the promised land is identified as the central issue, a sin of unbelief that manifests in both omission and commission.

The wilderness generation's self-enclosed estimation of their own prospects, rather than a posture of active receptivity towards God, reveals a fundamental brokenness in the human self. Their decision to turn back and wander in the wilderness, rather than pressing forward in faith, serves as a powerful illustration of the curvature of the self inward upon itself.

This crookedness, this inward curvature of the self, is a departure from the original design and a failure to image God rightly. Sin, in its varied expressions, mangles the way we were made to depend upon and reflect the divine. The wilderness generation serves as an emblem of this sinfulness, a cautionary tale that reminds us of the constant vigilance required to avoid the same pitfalls.

The pervasiveness of sin and its disordering effects on the human condition have been a central focus in Christian anthropology, particularly in the thought of Augustine of Hippo. Augustine's insights on the depth and universality of sin have been highly influential, shaping the way many Christians understand the fallen state of humanity.

However, it is important to note that an over-emphasis on the crooked self, to the exclusion of the created self, can lead to a reductive and pessimistic view of the human condition. While the scriptural witness to the profound impact of sin must be taken seriously, it is equally vital to maintain an appreciation for the beauty of God's original creation and the inherent goodness of the human person.

The Resurrected Self: Union with Christ and New Identity

The story of humanity's restoration, however, does not end in enmity, for God intervenes with his transformative grace. Through the saving work of Jesus Christ, the dying self is displaced, and the Christian self is resurrected, marked by a new orientation and a new identity.

Galatians 2 provides a powerful illustration of this transformation, as the apostle Paul addresses the fundamental issues of identity and belonging. In Christ, the Jew-Gentile distinction is relativized, for all identities are crucified, and a new life is born. The Christian self is defined not by the passions of the flesh or the desires of the body and mind, but by the love and blessing of the Son of God.

This Christological reorientation is not merely a matter of justification, but a deeper union with Christ that gives rise to a new, eccentric self. The self is directed toward and connected with the death and life of Jesus, resulting in a profound transformation that draws the self outward, away from its former curved inwardness.

The concept of union with Christ is a central tenet of Pauline theology and has been a crucial aspect of Christian anthropology throughout the centuries. In this union, the believer's identity is wholly bound to the person and work of Jesus, leading to a fundamental re-centering of the self around the reality of the new creation in Christ.

The Transfigured Self: Divine Delight and the Particularities of Grace

The narrative of redemption, however, does not end with the resurrected self, for the scriptures depict an even more glorious vision of the transfigured self. The Christological work of salvation not only reorients the self, but also transfigures the particular character and specific actions of the Christian, which become worthy of divine delight.

The Song of Songs, with its sensual and startling imagery, bears witness to this divine joy, as the Christ figure delights in the bride, the church. This transformed self is not a mere toleration of human form and nature, but a celebration of the creaturely image of God's own Son, where grace and nature meet in a beautiful tapestry.

This vision of the transfigured self challenges reductive views of Christology that limit the redemptive change wrought in Christ to solely justifying or substitutionary aspects. The wider scope of new creation, wherein our identity is wholly bound to union with Christ, demands attention. In this union, our created and natural specificity is transfigured, becoming worthy of divine delight.

The church's mission to offer care and comfort to souls, both inside and outside its fold, requires a robust Christology that attends not only to justification but also to the transformative gift of glory. Christ assumes our plight, walks our path, and secures our glory and blessing. He delights in the distinct particularities he has created and recreated through his gracious power.

Implications for Christian Identity and Ministry

The comprehensive understanding of the Christian self – the created, the crooked, the resurrected, and the transfigured – offers a nuanced perspective on the human condition and the work of God's grace. This breadth of biblical and theological elements is essential for grasping the complexity of Christian identity.

Two key implications emerge from this exploration. First, we must beware of a reductive Augustinian anthropology that views humanity solely through the prism of sin, neglecting the equally vital aspect of created goodness. While Augustinian insights on the pervasiveness of sin and its disordering effects must be taken seriously, they must be balanced with an appreciation for the beauty of God's handiwork and the inherent worth of the human person.

Second, we must guard against reductive views of Christology that limit the redemptive change wrought in Christ to solely justifying or substitutionary aspects. The wider scope of new creation, wherein our identity is wholly bound to union with Christ, demands attention. In this union, our created and natural specificity is transfigured, becoming worthy of divine delight.

The church's mission to offer care and comfort to souls, both inside and outside its fold, requires a robust Christology that attends not only to justification, but also to the transformative gift of glory. Christ assumes our plight, walks our path, and secures our glory and blessing. He delights in the distinct particularities he has created and recreated through his gracious power.

Attentiveness to the distinct, biblical sources of the Christian self is essential for appreciating the rich tapestry of Christian identity. By embracing the breadth of these anthropological elements, we can navigate the complexities of the human condition with wisdom and compassion, offering the transformative hope of the gospel to a world in need of restoration.

The Distinction of the Judaism Identity of Self

A dualistic understanding of humanity took root in some ancient Jewish communities, deeply affected by the principles of Greek philosophy. From this angle, the divine essence is associated with the immortal, intellectual soul, sharply contrasting with the body's physical nature. Various philosophers throughout history—both ancient and modern—shared this perspective, viewing the divine likeness in ethical dimensions, especially emphasizing the will's freedom. Yet, it becomes clear that one cannot delineate a singular doctrine concerning humanity merely from isolated biblical verses; rather, a thorough exploration of the biblical writings is necessary.

This holistic vision of human nature primarily influenced biblical thought; however, subtle shifts emerged within apocalyptic literature spanning from the 2nd century BCE to the 2nd century CE. The understanding of Nefesh began to evolve into an entity perceived as separable, a facet of existence that could exist outside the corporeal form. Even though such interpretations still echo biblical concepts, they introduced an emerging dualism prevalent in these texts. In Alexandrian Hellenistic Judaism, the assimilation of Greek philosophical tenets—particularly Plato's notions involving the soul's imprisonment by the body—gave rise to a clearer division that fostered a negative view of physical existence.

In contrast, rabbinic thought retained a closer alignment with the biblical understanding, highlighting humans as psychosomatic beings. This perspective acknowledged a body-soul dichotomy consistent with the prevailing belief in the temporary detachment of these elements upon

death. Biblical literature portrayed humanity as an inseparable psychosomatic unit, framing death as a dissolution rather than an obliteration.
While life ceases, this dissolution does not imply total annihilation.
Certain aspects of this vital force may persist yet must not be understood
as life in its full vibrancy. The ancient view of Sheol—the realm of the
dead—portrayed an existence devoid of lively interaction, signifying more
a shadowy echo of life. Most biblical authors depicted the dead as having
minimal to no awareness, indefinitely awaiting divine intervention to
ignite revival.

Interestingly, the conception of Sheol, alongside the belief in the
miraculous capacity for restoring the deceased to life and reviving exiled
Israel, underpinned the emerging ideas surrounding bodily resurrection
in the forthcoming age. Early Iranian religious concepts, illustrating a
cosmic confrontation with death eventually yielding to life through resurrection, likely influenced these Jewish ideologies. Although early inklings
of bodily resurrection surface in postexilic texts like Isaiah 26:19 and
Daniel 12:2, they imply that genuine life necessitates the reconstitution
of the psychosomatic unit. Such hopes were inherently intertwined with
Israel's eschatological aspirations and were believed to be reserved for the
righteous.

As subsequent apocalyptic literature unfolded, it fortified a heightened distinction between the body and spirit, suggesting that the soul
might exist independently in a disembodied state after death. Although
the doctrine of bodily resurrection endured, theological trajectories began
to shift. Souls were perceived as shades in Sheol, giving rise to beliefs
about personal survival linked to individual identities, influenced by the
individual-centric tendencies of Hellenistic thought. Consequently, the
notion of bodily resurrection appeared somewhat diminished; true life
after death was revised into a liberation from the limitations of the physical form, often overshadowing the concept of resurrection.

Nevertheless, the vital focus for biblical and rabbinic scholars
revolved not around the condition of the soul but rather on the ethical
implications related to humanity's composite nature. Scripture conveys
that humans live in a tension between the "heavenly" and the "earthly."

As such, human beings embody a unique capability of serving their Creator, empowered with the freedom to choose ethically amid these dualities. This ethical decision-making capacity stands as the hallmark of human existence, emerging not merely from the "heavenly" side but deeply rooted in humanity's intrinsic duality.

Within rabbinic discussions, this ethical dichotomy did not align with a simplistic body-soul dualism that cast the body in a negative light. Though occasionally surfacing in rabbinic literature intermixed with medieval mystical inquiries and philosophical debates, these insights represented earnest attempts to engage with the larger currents of thought and to confront the inherent tensions found even within earlier writings.

The Ethically Bound Creature

Humanity is fundamentally characterized as ethically engaged and responsible. The initial eleven chapters of Genesis predominantly highlight this responsibility regarding humankind's ability to choose between obedience and disobedience. Rabbinic Judaism broadened this discourse via the narrative of God's covenant with Noah (Genesis 9:8-17), establishing this covenant as a framework for humanity's ethical obligations. Viewed through this lens, all of humanity—rather than merely Israel—is seen in a covenantal relationship with God, articulated through numerous precepts devised to promote general humanitarian principles and to nurture an orderly society. The covenant made with Israel aimed to cultivate a community dedicated to fostering such societal advancement through their commitment and testimony.

In rabbinic thought, the ethical dimension of human nature draws not solely from the dynamic between the "heavenly" and "earthly." Still, it is also sculpted by the interplay of two primary "impulses." The biblical term yetzer, generally translated as "impulse" or "formation," emerges in two significant references within Genesis (6:5; 8:21). It depicts human inclination as ra'—potentially implying "evil" from a moral standpoint, yet equally interpretable as disordered. Other instances of the term lack this qualifier; however, traditional Aramaic translations often interpreted it as bisha ("wicked"). The rabbinical tradition introduced terms like ha-ra' ("the evil impulse") to represent disobedient inclinations, while yetzer ha-ṭov ("the good impulse") symbolized humanity's capacity for obedience. These concepts illustrate the ethical dynamics of human duality, while emphasizing the struggle between these opposing impulses, signifying freedom in making ethical choices.

Judaism affirms that genuine freedom resides in the ethical sphere, acknowledging the impacts and limitations of one's innate and circumstantial influences. Positioned within a covenantal backdrop, humans maintain the prerogative to act in obedience or rebel against divine authority. Thus, sin materializes as a conscious act of defiance against God's sovereign will. This theme holds particular weight in relation to Israel, where the covenantal relationship is expounded with greater detail. Nevertheless, the tradition posits that all humanity is enveloped within this divine covenant, embracing moral imperatives calling for ethical conduct, culminating in universally applicable choices.

The collective and individual acceptance of divine authority by the Israelites is encapsulated in the framework of "receiving the yoke of kingship." This acceptance comprises both an intellectual allegiance to essential beliefs, as articulated in the Deuteronomic affirmation: "Hear, O Israel, the Lord, our God, the Lord is one!"—and a commitment to uphold moral conduct at both individual and communal levels. Judaism holds these two responses as interconnected; thus, to reject divine authority signifies a denial of God's sovereignty both intellectually and practically, articulated as the act of "breaking the yoke of kingship."

Sin encompasses three interrelated themes: idolatry, murder, and illicit sexual conduct, each symbolizing rebellion against God's prescriptions. Such actions disrupt communal harmony, positioning individuals against one another and undermining God's design for establishing a perfected society.

If humans possess the freedom to embrace rebellion and must face its consequences, they equally carry the capacity to realign themselves toward reconciliation with God. The prophetic literature bursts with possibilities in this regard, even though the term teshuva ("turning") primarily appears in later rabbinic texts. This concept is fundamentally connected to the covenant: the opportunity for humanity to return to God remains intact, as divine commitment persists despite human shortcomings. Rabbinic thought emphasized that even dire prophecies of calamity imply a chance for repentance, motivated by remorse and a yearning for reconnection. This reconciliation possesses dual facets: divine readiness and human willingness.

Prophetic literature articulates immediate historical contexts threaded with geopolitical ramifications, increasingly resonating within synagogue liturgy infused with teachings from Torah and prophetic insights alike. The overarching divine summons reverberates consistently, inviting humanity to amend rebellion through constructive endeavors while encouraging restoration in both individual and community lives.

Following the catastrophic revolts against Rome, rabbinic leadership sought to reconstruct a devoted community through worship and active engagement within a structured society where individuals could lead lives tuned to divine expectations. Although specific paths towards this goal were not meticulously drafted, this generally represented a foundational framework for an eventual revitalization of humanity.

The Ethical Emphasis of Judaism

The intersection of affirmations about God and humanity in Jewish thought is effectively illustrated by the concept of Torah, which serves as the framework guiding human life in accordance with the divine. Humans, imbued with ethical responsibility, remain attuned to God's presence, which is evident in nature and historical occurrences. This responsiveness manifests on many levels, yet attains clearest articulation within interpersonal relationships, with the Pentateuch laying foundational principles for such engagements. Prophetic teachings underscore that neglecting these foundational ethics results in discord, both socially and personally, reinforcing the necessity for ethical considerations threaded through all societal layers.

Even revered figures within society are not exempt from ethical mandates. This dynamic is exemplified in Nathan's confrontation with King David following the latter's moral transgressions involving

Bathsheba—an arresting demonstration that ethical obligations traverse social hierarchies.

Jewish ethical models delineate that while God epitomizes the source of ethical imperatives, He concurrently serves as the archetype. The so-called Code of Holiness, explicated in Leviticus (19), frames emulating divine holiness as the foundation of human conduct, encompassing both ceremonial and ethical dimensions. The command, "You shall be holy, for I, the Lord your God, am Holy," underscores a moral framework concerning treatment of economically vulnerable populations, obligations towards neighbors, dignified conduct towards hired workers and the disabled, familial duties, and attitudes towards outsiders.

Both communal engagement and individual moral conduct are interwoven within Jewish ethical frameworks. A just society demands equitable individuals, and virtuous persons thrive within a just communal framework. Ethical mandates articulated through legal precepts target both dimensions, exemplifying that establishing a holy community and nurturing pious individuals coincide. This relationship oscillates with historical contexts, shifting focus from collective responsibilities to private ethical duties—particularly following the destruction of the Judaean state (70-135 CE), which often limited focus to non-political individual responsibilities.

The intertwining ethical commitments were especially pronounced in the biblical context, where divine mandates spanned both community and individual dimensions. In the rabbinic context, however, evolving political landscapes often prompted discussions to emphasize personal responsibilities, creating a distance from the governance of communal obligations. Regardless, the moral virtues manifesting in interpersonal relations inherently stem from original biblical foundations. Righteousness and compassion, initially established as responsibilities of civil governance, illuminate the relational dynamics between political entities, as illustrated in prophetic literature, wherein Micah's call to act justly and love mercy applies universally.

Emerging from the aftermath of the Jewish Diaspora, the individualistic ethical framework gained prominence, remaining without comprehensive systems of theoretical ethics until the Middle Ages. Importantly, reflections of ethical systems rooted themselves in the foundational practices of Halakhah (law), intending to encapsulate an ethical core that precedes revelation—asserting that divine laws inherently embody justice and mercy reflective of God's character.

Key Moral Virtues

Aligned with rabbinic interpretations of Torah, the domain of study is regarded as ethically virtuous. Texts from the Mishna recited in traditional prayer settings, enumerate numerous virtuous actions, including honoring parents, engaging in acts of loving-kindness, participating in regular worship rituals, extending hospitality, caring for the sick, providing for brides, ensuring dignified burial practices, dedicating oneself to prayer, and fostering peace within communities and families. These accumulate in proposing engagement with Torah study as the utmost ethical virtue.

The extensive ethical behaviors illustrated in the Mishna and liturgy testify to the numerous obligations inherent in Jewish tradition. Respecting familial harmony, parental accountability extends toward children, while marital obligations underscore reciprocal responsibilities between spouses. Biblical portrayals of God championing the vulnerable —like the fatherless and widows—remain pivotal in nurturing ethical conduct within a community. Concerns surrounding economic interactions find expression, too, as illustrated by commandments against unjust measurements (Leviticus 19:35-36) and the condemnation voiced by Amos against exploiting the righteous for personal gain (Amos 2:6). Collectively, these various injunctions contribute to a balanced framework of ethical behavior pertinent to both individuals and society at large.

Yet, ethical considerations extend beyond human relationships, delving into the very fibers of nature itself. The biblical ethos mandated compassion towards the animal kingdom; thus, observance of the Sabbath required rest not only for humans but also for domesticated animals (Exodus 20:10; 23:12). Prohibitions against animal mistreatment (Deuteronomy 22:4) and the destruction of wildlife (Deuteronomy 6-7) resonate distinctly with the commitment to responsible stewardship of creation. The rabbinic perspective amplifies this call, deeming it essential for humanity to contemplate obligations toward the entirety of nature, including conserving productive trees during sieges (Deuteronomy 20:14-20). This broad duty is encapsulated in the rabbinic directive, "You shall not destroy," which governs humanity's interaction with the environment.

The Distinction of the Islam Identity of Self

Uncovering the Self in Islam: The Pursuit of Self-Improvement, Self-Esteem, and Self-Awareness

This captivating exploration delves into the transformative power of self-discovery through the prism of Islamic teachings.

Within the profound realm of Islamic philosophy, pivotal ideas like self-exertion, self-esteem, and self-disregard arise as essential benchmarks for comprehending the multifaceted essence of the self. These interconnected concepts function as a roadmap, steering us through the diverse dimensions of the heart, spirit, and psyche.

At the core of this pursuit lies the essential act of self-contemplation, a potent catalyst for self-awareness and spiritual growth. The Quran's emphasis on introspection encourages believers to observe the signs of Allah's creation, a path to deeper understanding of themselves and their place in the expansive cosmos.

Their spiritual evolution directs them to fulfill their sacred purpose as per the precepts of Islam.

Muslims strive to attain deeper self-understanding, acknowledging their capacities, limitations, and opportunities for improvement. This endeavor not only cultivates personal progress, but also steers individuals toward their spiritual evolution, directing them to fulfill their sacred purpose as per the precepts of Islam. As we delve deeper into the journey of self-discovery, it becomes apparent that the Islamic identity transcends mere labels of ethnicity or culture; it embodies a profound spiritual evolution. This evolution necessitates a harmonious blend of individual effort and divine guidance, echoing the fundamental belief that self-improvement is not merely a personal endeavor, but a collective journey interwoven with the threads of faith.

Islam emphasizes the necessity of self-exertion, or "jihad al-nafs," translating to the struggle against one's own lower self. This inner struggle is not only a battle against negative impulses but also a vital part of cultivating virtues such as patience, humility, and compassion. The teachings of the Prophet Muhammad (peace be upon him) illuminate the path towards mastering oneself, urging the faithful to engage in constant reflection, thus enabling them to confront their flaws with courage and commitment. It is through this relentless self-assessment that believers can unearth their true potential, aligning their actions with the divine will.

Self-esteem, often misunderstood as mere self-importance, is intricately threaded with the Islamic perception of humility and servitude. In recognizing their worth as creations of Allah, individuals are called to forge a healthy self-esteem that does not inflate the ego, but rather enhances their sense of belonging and purpose. This balanced self-view allows Muslims to embrace their strengths while remaining meek in the face of their imperfections. The Quran addresses this beautifully, reminding us that each soul is crafted with unique qualities, each worthy of love, respect, and success, guiding individuals to find strength in their identity as worshipers of the One.

The journey of self-discovery is heavily influenced by the social fabric of the ummah, the global community of Muslims. The teachings of Islam encourage believers to forge connections with one another, reminding them that individual growth is intricately connected to the overall well-being of their community. Acts of kindness, charity, and empathy are not merely actions, but integral components of self-identity, reinforcing the idea that one's personal development is a reflection of their commitment to collective upliftment.

Thus, self-awareness in Islam becomes a dynamic interplay between the individual and the community, the self and the divine. By cultivating a deeper understanding of their own identities, Muslims are also called to advance the identities of those around them. This sense of interconnectedness fosters a robust framework for self-improvement – one that nurtures not just personal fulfillment, but also societal harmony.

In embracing the holistic vision of Islam, believers are inspired to reflect upon the transcendent nature of their identity. The continuous pursuit of knowledge, introspection, and compassion serves as a wellspring of empowerment, illuminating the pathway to realizing a purpose far greater than the self. By engaging with the profound teachings of their faith, Muslims embark on a sacred journey that leads them towards the ultimate destination: a life grounded in purpose, fulfillment, and unwavering belief in the mercy and guidance of Allah. It is by aligning the beliefs and perceptions of their perceived identity that they ultimately achieve their understanding of their identity.

EASTERN IDEOLOGY AND PHILOSOPHY

A Profound Path of Transformation: Exploring the Religious Dimensions of Buddhism

The question of whether Buddhism is a religion, psychology, or a way of life is a longstanding debate that has captivated scholars, practitioners, and the general public alike. At the heart of this discourse lies the complex and often contentious concept of what constitutes a religion. Is Buddhism a religion, psychology, or way of life?

The definition that resonates most is the one proposed by the late Buddhologist Frederick Streng, who described religion as "a means to ultimate transformation." This conceptualization recognizes the potential for personal growth and transcendence, without making judgments based on specific theological, practical, or ethical considerations. When viewed through this lens, Buddhism's rich offerings become increasingly clear.

Buddhism unequivocally presents an ultimate reality, whether it is termed nirvana, Buddhahood, or some other formulation. Across its diverse schools and sects, there is a shared notion of an absolute, transcendent state that lies beyond the confines of the mundane. Moreover, Buddhism provides a clear and distinct path for the individual to experience this ultimate reality, whether it be the Eightfold Path of Theravada, the bodhisattva journey of Mahayana, or other transformative practices.

Equally significant is the personal transformation that results from the experience of this ultimate reality. As Buddhologists observe, Buddhists who attain enlightenment demonstrate a profound shift in their ethics, behaviors, and overall manifestation of their Buddha-nature. This spiritual metamorphosis lies at the heart of Buddhism's religious dimension.

Yet, the perspectives on Buddhism's religious nature are not monolithic. Buddhologists offer a contrasting viewpoint, arguing that the Buddha's teachings were not intended to be a religion, but rather a "science of mind" – a method of investigation and exploration that empowers individuals to uncover the truth for themselves. Rinpoche suggests that when we approach the Buddha's wisdom as final, unquestionable answers, we risk practicing Buddhism as a religion, rather than as a transformative journey of self-discovery.

This distinction is crucial, as it highlights the delicate balance between the religious and the investigative aspects of the Buddhist path. The Buddha himself was not seeking religion, but rather the truth that could liberate him and all beings from suffering. His teachings, then, can be seen as a means to this ultimate freedom, rather than a set of dogmatic beliefs to be accepted on faith alone.

Buddhologist writing from the perspective of the Chan and Zen koan traditions, offers a nuanced perspective on Buddhism's relationship with religion. She suggests that the "religious event at the heart of the koan tradition is awakening, which reunites us with the sacred, or true, nature of things." In this view, the sacred text is not a fixed scripture, but rather the world itself, which we are constantly learning to interpret and engage with.

Buddhologist's conception of Buddhism as a "culture of awakening" rather than an organized religion resonates with other Buddhologist's emphasis on investigation and personal discovery. The koan tradition, with its conversations, stories, and commentaries, becomes a means to spark the revelatory experience of oneness with the universe, rather than a set of dogmas to be believed.

Ultimately, the question of whether Buddhism is a religion or not may not have a single, definitive answer. As preeminent Buddhologists have demonstrated, there are valid arguments on both sides of this discourse. What is clear, however, is that Buddhism offers a profound path of personal transformation, one that can be approached through a religious lens or as a rigorous, investigative exploration of the nature of mind and existence.

Within the traditional definitions of religion, Buddhism can indeed be considered a religion. It presents an ultimate reality, a distinct path to experiencing that reality, and a profound transformation of the individual. However, the diversity of perspectives within the Buddhist tradition itself reflects its adaptability and the richness of the human experience. Whether one views Buddhism as a religion, a philosophy, or a science of the mind, its core teachings continue to inspire, challenge, and guide countless individuals on their quest for greater understanding and freedom from suffering.

In this sense, the ongoing debate surrounding Buddhism's religious status may be less important than the transformative insights it offers to all who embark on this timeless journey. The diversity of views on the matter serves to highlight the multifaceted nature of this ancient wisdom tradition, inviting us to explore its depths with an open and curious mind.

THE DIFFERENCES IN EASTERN AND WESTERN PHILOSOPHIES OF THE SELF

In Western ideologies, the concept of an independent human self is upheld, while Eastern ideologies reject the notion of a fixed self. Eastern thought views "the self" as illusory, believing instead in the interconnectedness and influence of a larger entity or power beyond individual existence. Eastern religions emphasize the connection to a greater force, challenging the Western emphasis on individual identity. This philosophical contrast reflects differing perspectives on the nature of selfhood and the relationship between individuals and the broader universe. While Western beliefs focus on self-reliance and distinctiveness, Eastern philosophies highlight unity and a harmonious existence within a larger cosmic context. The divergent views on selfhood in these contrasting ideologies reveal deep-rooted cultural and philosophical differences in how human identity is perceived and understood.

Western Ideas of the Self

Individualistic

Prioritizes the value and independence of the individual over the group as a whole.

In a world where conformity and unity were highly prized, there was one individual who stood out for valuing independence above all else. His name was Ethan, a young man with a relentless spirit and a fierce determination to chart his own path, regardless of societal expectations.

While many in his community strived to blend in and maintain harmony within the group, Ethan thrived on pushing boundaries and exploring new horizons. He believed that true growth and fulfillment could only be achieved by following one's unique calling, even if it meant going against the grain.

Despite facing criticism and skepticism from those around him, Ethan remained steadfast in his belief that the value of one's individuality should never be sacrificed for the sake of conformity. He saw his independence as a source of strength, not a weakness, and he embraced it wholeheartedly.

As he ventured on his journey of self-discovery, Ethan inspired others to embrace their individuality and break free from the constraints of societal norms. He showed them that true freedom lay in being true to oneself, even if it meant standing alone at times.

And so, in a world that often favored the collective over the individual, Ethan emerged as a beacon of light for those who dared to dream and forge their own path. His unwavering belief in the value of independence served as a reminder that true greatness comes from honoring one's unique essence, no matter the cost.

- "The self" is a unique, personal identity separate from that of others.

During a lecture, my professor commenced an intriguing discussion on the uniqueness of Self. As he eloquently outlined his thoughts, I found myself nodding in agreement, fully engrossed in his words. The concept of "the self" had always fascinated me, sparking a profound curiosity about our individual identities. As the lecture continued, I found myself pondering the ways in which we define ourselves in the vast tapestry of existence. It was like peering into a mirror, trying to discern the intricate layers that made up my sense of self. With each passing moment, I delved deeper into the enigma of personal identity, marveling at the complexity and richness of the human experience. In that shared classroom, surrounded by eager minds hungry for knowledge, I felt a sense of unity in our collective quest to understand the essence of who we are. And as I left the lecture hall that day, I carried with me a newfound appreciation for the boundless depths of the self, that mysterious and ever-evolving portrait of our innermost being.

- Self-Identity has no inherent connection with the universe.

As a renowned philosopher once said, one's self-identity is not intertwined with the vast expanse of the universe. It stands alone, a distinct entity that is shaped by personal experiences, beliefs, and perceptions. Our existence is not dependent on the cosmos, but rather on the intricate fabric of our inner thoughts and emotions.

In the quest for self-discovery, we journey through the depths of our minds, seeking to unravel the mysteries that define who we are. It is a solitary pursuit, a voyage of introspection and reflection that leads us to the core of our being.

Through moments of clarity and moments of doubt, we forge our identity, carving out a unique path in the tapestry of existence. The stars do not dictate our essence, but by the choices we make and the values we hold dear.

So, let us embrace the beauty of our individuality, recognizing that our self-identity is a tapestry woven from the threads of our own lives. It is a precious gift, a reflection of our innermost truths that shines brightly in the infinite expanse of the universe.

Eastern Ideas of Self

Collectivistic: Prioritize the group as a whole rather than a single individual

This analogy illuminates this concept.

As they sailed across the vast ocean, the crew of The Unity knew their mission was not just about personal gain, but a collective effort to secure a better future for their people. Each member understood the importance of prioritizing the group as a whole, setting aside individual desires for the greater good.

Captain Lysandra led by example, always putting the well-being of her crew above her own. She made sure everyone was well-fed and rested, fostering a sense of unity and camaraderie among the sailors. It was this collective spirit that kept The Unity strong even in the face of fierce storms and daunting challenges.

When they finally reached the fabled island of New Horizons, the crew worked together seamlessly to build their new settlement. Every decision was made with the group in mind, ensuring that everyone had a voice in shaping their future. The sense of collectivism empowered each member to strive for the common goal, knowing that their efforts would benefit not just themselves, but all who called The Unity home.

Years passed, and The Unity prospered, its success a testament to the power of collectivism. Other ships would come and go, but none could match the unwavering unity of Captain Lysandra and her crew. Together, they had forged a community where every individual was valued, where the needs of the group always trumped those of the few.

And so, as the sun set on another day in paradise, The Unity stood strong, a shining beacon of what could be achieved when individuals set aside their differences and worked together for the greater good.

"The self" is an illusion.

The concept of the self as an illusion suggests that our sense of "self" is merely a focal point for our current subjective experiences. Certain aspects of this self may appear consistent enough over time to create the illusion of permanence, but they are actually just reflections of the various experiences we go through. This idea highlights the inter-connected nature of the self with the universe, illustrating how our sense of identity is not rigid and independent, but rather fluid and influenced by the interactions we have with the world around us. It invites us to explore the complexities of our existence and the subtle interplay between ourselves and the larger cosmic fabric of the universe.

Eastern Philosophy of the Self

A Comparison of Hinduism and Buddhism

Both Hinduism and Buddhism offer unique perspectives on the concept of the self, rooted in Eastern philosophy and spirituality. In Hinduism, the self is understood through the concepts of Brahman and Atman. Brahman is the divine essence that encompasses all beings in the universe and is responsible for creation, maintenance, and destruction. Atman, on the other hand, is the eternal soul of an individual that continues after the body dies and is believed to be reincarnated into another form. This belief system emphasizes the interconnectedness of all souls, likening them to rivers that ultimately flow into the same lake, representing the unity of Brahman.

Hindus strive for self-realization, seeking to merge their individual Atman with the universal consciousness of Brahman in order to achieve liberation. This process involves understanding and embracing one's true self as part of the greater whole, as described in the ancient Hindu text as "That art Thou". Unlike Western philosophy, which often views the self as an individual entity separate from others, Hinduism highlights the interconnected nature of existence, where each individual soul is seen as a part of the divine essence.

In contrast, Buddhism, founded by Siddhartha Gautama, who became known as the Buddha after attaining enlightenment, offers a different perspective on the concept of self. Buddhism emphasizes interconnectedness and the absence of a permanent self. According to Buddhist teachings, the idea of the self is an illusion, as individuals are perceived as streams of consciousness that are deeply interconnected with one another and with all existence. This interconnectedness negates the existence of a separate, individual self in the Buddhist framework.

Buddhists believe that because everything is interconnected, there is no distinct self that can exist independently from the whole. This concept is illustrated by the analogy of rivers flowing into a lake, where the water from the lake merges with that of the rivers, creating one continuous body of water. In Buddhism, the absence of an independent self, or Atman, is a fundamental principle that challenges the notion of individual identity and emphasizes the unity of all beings.

While Hinduism and Buddhism both offer profound insights into the nature of the self and the interconnectedness of existence, they diverge in their perspectives on the individual self. Hinduism sees the self as a part of the divine essence of Brahman, aiming for self-realization and unity with the universal consciousness. In contrast, Buddhism challenges the concept of a permanent self, emphasizing the impermanent and interconnected nature of all beings. Through these differing perspectives, both religions invite contemplation on the nature of the self and its place within the broader fabric of existence.

The concept of "the self" is approached differently in Western and Eastern philosophies. In the Western perspective, "the self" is viewed as an individual entity separate from others. On the other hand, Eastern ideologies consider "the self" as an illusion, emphasizing the interconnectedness of all beings.

In Hinduism, the relationship between Brahman, the soul of God, and Atman, the human soul, defines "the self". Atman is believed to be a part of Brahman, highlighting the interconnected nature of existence. The famous Hindu saying "That art Thou" encapsulates this connection between the human soul and the divine.

Similarly, Buddhism teaches that everything and everyone is interconnected, forming a greater whole. There is a constant interplay between entities, blurring the lines of individuality. In the Buddhist faith, the absence of a distinct self is emphasized, as our consciousness is intertwined with the fabric of existence.

Both Hinduism and Buddhism emphasize the unity and interconnectedness of all beings, challenging the Western notion of a separate and distinct self. These contrasting views offer diverse perspectives on the nature of identity and consciousness.

THE CONCEPT OF THE SELF IN BUDDHISM IS REFERRED TO AS MAYA

Maya, the elusive concept that challenges our understanding of the self in Buddhism. Like a tangled web of illusions, Maya reminds us that the self is not what it appears to be. It is a veil that distorts our perception of reality, leading us to believe in a false sense of identity.

In the teachings of Buddhism, Maya is often described as the root cause of suffering. It is the attachment to the illusion of self that keeps us trapped in the cycle of birth and death. By unraveling the layers of Maya, we can glimpse the true nature of reality - a vast emptiness that transcends individual identity.

Through meditation and mindfulness practices, one can begin to peel away the layers of Maya and uncover the true self that lies beneath. It is a journey of self-discovery and liberation, freeing oneself from the confines of ego and attachment.

Maya serves as a reminder that the self is not static or fixed, but rather a fluid and ever-changing phenomenon. By embracing the teachings of Maya, we can cultivate a deeper sense of compassion, wisdom, and interconnectedness with all beings.

So, next time you find yourself caught up in the illusions of the self, remember Maya - the ever-present reminder that true liberation comes from letting go of the self and embracing the boundless nature of our interconnected reality.

Maya, the artful architect of perception, the weaver of intricate illusions that entwine our minds in a dance of light and darkness, purity and passion, ignorance and enlightenment—its enigmatic presence casts a shadow over our very existence, beckoning us to break free from the shackles of illusion and embrace the radiant truth that lies at the core of our being.

As we delve deeper into the essence of Maya, the illusion of self becomes more apparent. Maya, described as the creative force intertwined with light, purity, activity, passion, ignorance, and darkness, embodies the intricate tapestry of human consciousness. It serves as the veil that shrouds our true nature, obscuring the essence of our being with illusions and distortions. The concept of Maya challenges us to question the authenticity of our perceptions and the reality we believe to be true.

In unraveling the layers of Maya, we confront the duality of existence – the constant interplay between what is perceived and what truly is. The illusion of self is intricately woven into the fabric of Maya, blurring the boundaries between our external persona and our inner essence. It beckons us to dive deep into the depths of our consciousness, peeling back the layers of conditioning and societal constructs that have shaped our sense of identity.

As we venture further along this enigmatic path, we come face to face with the complexities of the human experience. Each step forward reveals a new facet of our being, a revelation that challenges our preconceived notions and forces us to reconsider the nature of reality itself. The kaleidoscope of emotions and thoughts swirl around us, inviting us to embrace the uncertainty and embrace the paradoxes that lie at the heart of Maya.

In this dance of shadows and light, we begin to sense a deeper connection to the world around us, a profound awareness that transcends the limitations of our individual selves. The boundaries that once defined us fade away, merging with the infinite expanse of existence that stretches out before us. We become like a drop of water in the vast ocean, losing ourselves in the ebb and flow of the cosmic tide.

And as we surrender to this grand tapestry of illusion and truth, we find liberation in embracing the paradoxical nature of our existence. No longer confined by the constraints of duality, we become free to explore the boundless potential that lies within us. In this moment of revelation, we realize that the key to unlocking the mysteries of Maya lies not in deciphering its secrets, but in embracing the wonder and awe that it inspires within us.

Through the lens of Maya, we are invited to embark on a profound journey of self-discovery and introspection. It challenges us to shed the masks we wear and embrace the raw authenticity of our being. By transcending the illusions of self, we open ourselves to a higher state of awareness and enlightenment.

Maya, as the creative force and motherly love, guides us towards a deeper understanding of ourselves and the interconnectedness of all existence. It beckons us to look beyond the superficial and perceive the underlying unity that binds us all. As we navigate the labyrinth of Maya, we are called to embrace the uncertainties, the mysteries, and the infinite possibilities that lie within.

In embracing Maya and unraveling the illusion of self, we embark on a transformative journey towards self-realization and enlightenment. It is through this process of self-discovery that we can transcend the limitations of our ego and awaken to the profound beauty of our true essence. The illusion of self dissipates, and we are left with the radiant truth of our being, shining brightly in the cosmic tapestry of Maya.

The Rigveda, an ancient collection of Vedic Sanskrit hymns from India, delves into the intriguing concept of Maya, which refers to the gods' ability to manifest visible forms. As depicted in the Upanishads, Maya is portrayed as a potent energy or capacity inherent in God, known as Ishvara. However, as the ideals evolved in the Vedanta school texts, Maya took on a different interpretation, representing "illusion" or "illusory existence."

In the later stages of Vedic literature, particularly in the Upanishads, the enigmatic concept of Maya continued to captivate the minds of scholars and sages. With a subtle shift in interpretation, Maya transitioned from being seen as a divine creative force to embodying a deeper, more complex layer of existence. It began to be perceived as a veil that obscures the true nature of reality, leading individuals to perceive the multiplicity and diversity of the world as real, while, in essence, it is merely a transient illusion.

The Vedanta school of thought further delved into this profound philosophical idea, emphasizing that Maya is the deceptive power that veils the true self, Atman, and perpetuates the cycle of birth and death. In this school of thought, the ultimate goal of spiritual seekers was to transcend Maya's illusionary nature and realize the inherent unity of all existence.

Through intricate philosophical discourses and introspective contemplation, the scholars of Vedanta sought to unravel the mysteries of Maya and penetrate the veils of illusion that shroud the essence of reality. As they delved deeper into the nature of Maya, they also explored the concepts of Brahman, the ultimate reality, and the interconnectedness of all beings within this cosmic web of existence.

The evolution of the concept of Maya within the Vedic texts showcases the profound intellectual and spiritual journey undertaken by ancient sages and philosophers as they grappled with the fundamental questions of existence, illusion, and ultimate reality. It serves as a testament to the enduring quest for truth and enlightenment that has permeated the fabric of Indian philosophical thought for centuries.

In the realm of Buddhism, Maya retains its essence of "illusion," yet with a profound divergence in perspective. According to Buddhist teachings, the concept of inherent existence is debunked, leading to the assertion that Maya lacks the foundational basis to create illusory reflections. Within Buddhist philosophy, the absence of a definitive eternal or limitless substance or cause is emphasized. Life is envisioned as a dynamic interplay of fleeting elements intricately interconnected in an ever-flowing succession. This succession is closely entwined with the intricate twelvefold chain of causality, known as pratityasamutpada. Through the lens of Buddhist philosophy, every experience unfolds as a sequence of transient amalgamations, thereby revealing the illusory nature of the perceived continuity of existence.

It is fascinating to observe the different interpretations and applications of the concept of Maya across various ancient Indian philosophical traditions. In the Rigveda, Maya is depicted as a divine ability of the gods to manifest visible forms, showcasing a sense of creative power and illusion. Moving on to the Upanishads, Maya is perceived as an energy of God, adding a layer of complexity to its meaning.

However, as we delve into the Buddhist perspective on Maya, a distinct understanding emerges. Here, Maya is acknowledged as an illusion but takes on a deeper essence due to the fundamental belief in the absence of inherent existence. Within Buddhist philosophy, the concept of Maya is devoid of the capacity to create illusory reflections, with the absence of substantial foundations for such illusions.

In this philosophical outlook, life is seen as a dynamic and interconnected interplay of transient elements, rejecting the notion of eternal or boundless substances. The intricate web of causality, as depicted in the twelvefold chain of pratityasamutpada, is a profound and nuanced concept that lies at the heart of Buddhist thought. This interconnected sequence of causal relationships not only elucidates the nature of existence but also offers a profound understanding of the human condition and the means to transcend the cycle of suffering.

At the core of this intricate tapestry is the notion of dependent origination, the fundamental principle that all phenomena arise and exist in dependence upon multiple causative factors. This idea is encapsulated in the first two links of the pratityasamutpada: ignorance and karmic formations. Ignorance, the root cause of suffering, is the lack of understanding of the true nature of reality, while karmic formations are the volitional actions that perpetuate the cycle of rebirth.

From these initial conditions, the chain of causality unfolds, with consciousness arising from the karmic formations, the six sense bases, contact, feeling, craving, clinging, and becoming. This culminates in the final two links: birth and old age and death, the inevitable conclusion of the cycle of existence.

The profound insight of the pratityasamutpada lies in its ability to illustrate the interconnectedness of all phenomena, where a single event or condition can have far-reaching consequences, both in the present and the future. By understanding this intricate web of causality, the individual can begin to recognize the impermanent and conditional nature of existence, and thus cultivate the wisdom and compassion necessary to break free from the bondage of suffering.

Through the careful contemplation of the pratityasamutpada, the seeker can uncover the root causes of their suffering and gradually uproot the conditions that perpetuate the cycle of rebirth. By fostering a deep understanding of the causal relationships that govern the human experience, one can then actively work to transform the very conditions that give rise to suffering, illustrating the impermanent and interconnected nature of existence. Through this lens, the continuity of life is perceived as illusory, unraveling the depths of Maya in the realm of Buddhist philosophy.

The idea of Maya as impermanence leads to the Buddhist notion of individuality as a stream of transitory states of consciousness (Santana). Accepting the premise of impermanence makes the law of causality or dependent origination possible. It forms the link between the existent and the non-existent or the Middle Path, between the two extremes of eternalism and nihilism. The Middle Path in Buddhism can be juxtaposed with the relation between Brahman and Maya in the tradition of Vedanta.

The concept of Maya as impermanence in Buddhism finds its roots in the idea of individuality being a continuous stream of fleeting states of consciousness. Embracing the notion of impermanence lays the foundation for the law of causality or dependent origination to take place. This connection serves as the bridge between the tangible and intangible, known as the Middle Path, steering clear of the extremes of eternalism and nihilism. The Middle Path in Buddhist philosophy can be likened to the intricate relationship between Brahman and Maya in the teachings of Vedanta.

In Theravada Buddhism, the philosophical aspect of Maya is given little importance apart from its use as the name of Buddha's mother. In Mahayana Buddhism, Maya plays a vital role in connecting to its meaning of "illusion" and the fundamental teaching of emptiness. Due to ignorance, objects can be considered to exist independently of causes and conditions, which hinders the possibility of recognizing their true essence as empty and as a magical manifestation.

In Vajrayana Buddhism, Maya's significance continues to be deeply intertwined with the concept of illusion and emptiness. Within this branch of Buddhism, practitioners delve into the intricate layers of Maya, recognizing that all phenomena are inherently devoid of inherent existence. Through rigorous practices and teachings, Vajrayana followers strive to penetrate the illusion of Maya and perceive the ultimate reality beyond superficial appearances. This deep understanding of Maya serves as a gateway to unlocking the true nature of existence and attaining enlightenment.

Vajrayana Buddhism focuses on the same idea but in a different way. The completion stage of Tantric practice includes achieving a kind of union with a particular deity's illusory body (may deva), similar to a magical illusion. This practice aims at attaining liberation from the existence of objects and the duality of samsara and nirvana.

Exploring the intricacies of Vajrayana Buddhism reveals a unique approach to achieving spiritual enlightenment. While sharing similarities with other Buddhist practices, Vajrayana delves into the concept of union with a deity's illusory body. This mystical union with the deity's form, akin to a mesmerizing magical illusion, forms the essence of the completion stage in Tantric practice.

Through this profound practice, practitioners aspire to transcend the boundaries of worldly existence, ultimately seeking liberation from the dualistic nature of samsara and nirvana. The union with the deity's illusory body represents a path towards realizing a deeper understanding of the illusory nature of our perceived reality, guiding individuals towards a state of profound spiritual awakening.

The typical Buddhist viewpoint holds that everything in life is an illusion. According to Buddhist perceptions, life itself can be considered a manifestation of mahamaya, the grand illusion—the mother of all existing things. The name of the mother of the Buddha, the goddess Maya, points to the illusory character of his birth, of birth itself, of life. It unites philosophical concepts across the Buddhist spectrum and embodies the Dharma's message. On the one hand, the name Maya has a negative connotation, expressed by the force of delusion, which binds people to the cycle of existence. However, on the other hand, it also carries the positive meaning of a creative power associated with motherly love: the most potent force on earth.

Expanding on the concept of mahamaya, it is believed that the illusions we encounter throughout our lives serve as opportunities for spiritual growth and enlightenment. By recognizing and accepting the ephemeral nature of existence, one can transcend worldly attachments and achieve a deeper understanding of the interconnectedness of all things. The duality of Maya as both a deceptive force and a nurturing presence mirrors the complexities of human experience. Embracing this paradox can lead to profound insight and inner peace, guiding individuals on their spiritual journey towards ultimate truth and liberation from suffering. Through contemplation of mahamaya, one can awaken to the boundless essence of existence and tread the path towards enlightenment with clarity and compassion.

Humans are engulfed in their daily lives, created by their minds and perceived as reality. This reality gives little thought or realization of who we really are, why we are here, where we are going, what our purpose is, or even what meaning our life has. Most of us have never realized what the term "true self" actually is or given much thought to the soul and the purpose it plays in the human body. The idea of the soul is called Anattā in Buddhism, which is described as the doctrine that there is in humans no permanent, underlying substance that can be called the soul. Humans are engulfed in their daily lives, created by their minds and perceived as reality.

As we navigate through the hustle and bustle of our daily routines, it's easy to get lost in the sea of tasks and responsibilities that make up our perceived reality. Many of us seldom pause to ponder the deeper questions that lie beneath the surface – questions about our true essence, our reason for existence, and the mysteries of the soul that dwell within us.

In the realm of Buddhism, the concept of Anattā sheds light on the notion that there is no enduring, unchanging essence within us that can be labeled as the soul. This doctrine challenges us to look beyond the tangible aspects of our being and delve into the profound complexity of our true nature.

As we navigate through the depths of our consciousness, we are confronted with the realization that our identity is not confined to a static entity but rather a fluid and interconnected web of experiences, thoughts, and emotions. Embracing the concept of Anattā invites us to release our attachment to the illusion of a permanent self and to cultivate a deeper understanding of impermanence and interconnectedness. Through this ancient wisdom, we are encouraged to embark on a journey of self-discovery and liberation, transcending the limitations of the ego and embracing the infinite possibilities that lie within the boundless expanse of our consciousness.

Amidst the chaos of our external lives, perhaps it's in exploring the depths of our inner world that we may uncover the essence of our existence and the interconnectedness of all things. Embracing the fluidity and impermanence of our being, we might just catch a glimpse of the profound beauty that lies within the infinite layers of our true selves.

Humans are often perceived as limited beings, primarily composed of physical bodies and mere living organisms. Within this perception, we tend to exist and thrive within fear-based realities, whether consciously or unconsciously. The self-structure we so closely identify with, our physical body, is inherently finite and will eventually cease to exist.

In contemporary society, a significant portion of individuals who engage in religious, spiritual, or ideological practices often do so within a framework conditioned by egoic culture. The techniques they employ may inadvertently reinforce the illusion of the ego, perpetuating a cycle of seeking external validation. The belief that adherence to certain ideologies or practices will provide ultimate answers about one's identity is a fundamental flaw that fosters narrow thinking.

Spirituality, as commonly practiced, mirrors pathological patterns of thought prevalent in society. It can be seen as a heightened form of mental agitation, urging individuals towards constant doing rather than being. This continual pursuit of external validation through wealth, power, or love perpetuates the ego construct, fueling an insatiable craving for attainment. As the cycles of desire and dissatisfaction weave through the fabric of society, the true essence of spirituality becomes shrouded in illusion. Instead of seeking liberation from the confines of the ego, many find themselves entangled in a web of expectations and comparisons. The pursuit of enlightenment is reduced to a commodity, a status symbol to be displayed rather than a journey of self-discovery.

In essence, the quest for self-discovery and fulfillment is noble, but the reliance on external sources for validation perpetuates a cycle of spiritual materialism that overlooks the essence of true being. It is essential to transcend the egoic constructs and recognize that true contentment lies not in external acquisitions but in embracing the present moment with a sense of inner peace and acceptance. A significant goal that one attains or, literally, "makes actual" or "makes real" on one's mental continuum. The common actual attainments, shared with non-Buddhists, refer to extraphysical powers (the eight actual attainments), while the supreme actual attainment refers to enlightenment.

SPIRITUAL PATH AND THE EGOIC CONSTRUCT

Those treading the spiritual path strive to shift their focus away from the ego construct and immerse themselves in spiritual aspects. It's crucial to recognize the potential danger that lies in desiring to become more awakened or enlightened as you absorb these words. The inclination to attain enlightenment is often driven by the ego construct, which thrives on desires for acquisition and self-enhancement. True awakening does not involve accumulating more or seeking external validation. Instead, it entails learning to let go of attachments and embracing the concept of dying before physical death occurs.

Life and death form an inseparable continuum, much like yin and yang, endlessly intertwining without a clear beginning or end. By resisting the natural flow of life and avoiding the inevitability of death, we inadvertently inhibit our capacity to experience truth without the distortions imposed by the ego fully. When one transcends the ego's influence, fear of life and death dissipates, paving the way for profound acceptance and understanding.

Our upbringing and societal norms often instill values and beliefs that shape our perceptions and decisions. Beneath these conscious influences lie deep-seated biological impulses that govern our subconscious behaviors and responses. The ego construct essentially represents a cycle of repetition—a familiar path that our energy is predisposed to follow, whether it is beneficial or detrimental to our well-being. Memories upon memories, spiraling within spirals, influence our consciousness and tether us to societal conditioning, often referred to metaphorically as the "matrix."

While certain aspects of the ego can be recognized and integrated into our awareness, it's the unconscious, primal fears, and ingrained patterns of thought that predominantly steer our actions and shape our reality. We become entrapped in cycles of desire for pleasure, aversion to pain, and avoidance of discomfort, leading to detrimental behavioral patterns and self-imposed limitations. Through our work, relationships, beliefs, ideologies, and daily interactions, we unknowingly feed the ego construct, perpetuating a cycle of passive submission.

Many individuals move through life constrained by narrow patterns of existence, enduring significant suffering that is often self-inflicted. Breaking free from these conditioned paths rarely crosses their minds, as they remain oblivious to the possibility of choosing a different way. Liberation entails releasing the inherited past and aligning with the universal energy that propels us toward authentic self-expression and conscious living. Just as we were born into a world with biological predispositions but without self-awareness, shedding the layers of societal conditioning and false identities can lead to a profound awakening.

In the clarity of a child's gaze, devoid of the complexities of the fabricated self, lies a reminder of the luminous emptiness that we lose touch with as we mature. Shakespeare aptly likened life to a stage, where we play various roles, shedding light on the transient nature of personas and the illusory self. True awakening emerges when consciousness transcends the confines of personal identity, allowing one to discern the difference between the character they portray and their authentic essence. By surrendering to the guidance of universal energy, masks fall away, revealing the radiant truth at the core of our being.

In this journey towards spiritual awakening, the first step often involves recognizing the myriad ways in which the ego asserts its influence over our lives. The ego thrives on dichotomy: success versus failure, joy versus sorrow, belonging versus isolation. It constructs a reality where one's self-worth is contingent upon external assessments—how others perceive, validate, or criticize. Such a constructed reality manifests as a prison of self-judgment, hindering the pure essence of our spirit from revealing itself.

To dismantle this structure, one must embark on a path of introspection and honesty, unraveling the threads of conditioning that cling tightly to our lives. This process asks for courage—a brave willingness to face uncomfortable truths, all those hidden fears and regrets that have been buried under layers of defense mechanisms and coping strategies. Many resist this confrontation, fearing what truths may emerge from the shadows of the psyche. Yet, it is precisely in this excavation of the self that true transformation begins.

Meditation serves as a vital tool in this reclamation journey. By quieting the mind and turning inward, one may begin to witness the incessant chatter of the ego without attachment. It transforms the observer into an active participant in their inner landscape, providing insights into the patterns that perpetuate suffering. Viewing these thoughts as transient phenomena can foster a sense of detachment, allowing us to realize that we are not our thoughts, nor the stories the ego spins. In this space of observation, light begins to seep into the corners of our consciousness, illuminating the false narratives we unconsciously perpetuate.

As one begins to embrace the simplicity of being in the present moment, the relentless pursuit for more—more accolades, more love, more possessions—starts to fade into the background. The need to fortify the ego's facade diminishes, replaced by a profound appreciation of existence itself. Each breath taken becomes an affirmation of life, each moment an opportunity for mindful presence. This mindful presence cultivates gratitude for both the ordinary and extraordinary aspects of life, allowing one to forge connections not just with oneself but also with the wider universe.

Authenticity, born from this transformative journey, beckons us to align with our true values instead of inherited ones. The societal frameworks that dictate measures of success begin to crumble when one recognizes their transient nature, giving way to a deeper understanding of fulfillment that transcends materiality. An authentic existence resonates with the essence of interconnectedness; it fosters compassion, empathy, and understanding, bridging the gaps created by the ego's insistence on separation.

This journey is not static; it evolves continuously. Every experience—be it joyous or painful—serves as a catalyst for growth. In learning to embrace discomfort as part of the experience, the individual develops resilience and strength. The realization dawns that even in sorrow, there exists a wealth of wisdom. The darker emotions, often shunned or ignored, carry valuable lessons that deepen our understanding of the human experience. In essence, the acceptance of the full spectrum of emotions leads to greater authenticity; an acceptance that permits the spirit to flow unimpeded.

Through such acceptance arises the profound realization that we are part of a vast tapestry of existence. Each thread, each individual life, carries unique color and texture while contributing to the broader design. Within this understanding lies liberation—the illusion of separation dissipates, and we begin to recognize that we are mere players in a larger cosmic dance. The act of surrendering to this dance invites grace, allowing us to navigate the currents of life with an open heart and an attuned spirit.

Ultimately, the spiritual path leads to integration—where the dichotomy of self dissolves, revealing the whole. This wholeness manifests not as a destination, but as an ongoing journey of discovery and exploration. Every step taken in awareness propels us closer to the essence of our being, unfurling the petals of our innate wisdom and reconnecting us to the source from whence we came. True awakening becomes a daily practice of remembering, an invitation to live life fully, authentically, and with the unwavering trust in the inherent beauty and connectivity of all things.

THE DISCONNECT BETWEEN THE EGO AND SPIRITUALITY

The confluence of spiritual pursuits and the tendencies of the ego manifests in complex ways, often blurring the lines between genuine spiritual growth and egoic enhancement. The phenomenon of "spiritual bypassing," wherein individuals utilize spiritual beliefs as a means to sidestep personal or emotional issues, highlights this disconnect. While the individual may appear to be engaged in spiritual practice, they are often merely reinforcing the ego's facade, avoiding confrontation with the self and neglecting the critical work required for true emotional healing.

Charles Whitfield, in his book "Healing the Child Within," delineates how the ego often masquerades as enlightenment when, in fact, it may simply be an elevation of past traumas reinterpreted through a spiritual lens. Such transformations lack depth and authenticity, instead serving to enhance the identity rather than dissolve it. The allure of spiritual labels or achievements can exacerbate this issue, enticing individuals to cling to their ego's sense of superiority. This creates a paradox where the quest for enlightenment entangles itself further in the very structures it seeks to dismantle.

Additionally, the Western commodification of spirituality has generated an environment where spiritual practices are synthesized into lifestyle choices. This "spiritual consumerism" can dilute genuine practices into marketable items, like yoga retreats, healing crystals, or mindfulness apps, leading to a form of superficial engagement that often fails to address the deeper psychological wounds. Spirituality becomes yet another arena for the ego to exert its influence, emphasizing trends rather than transformation.

The Role of Relationships in Ego Dissolution

Relationships serve as one of the most profound mirrors reflecting our egoic patterns. The dynamics we engage in with others reveal our attachments, fears, and coping mechanisms. Love and connection become potent forces in this journey; however, they also represent potential traps for egoic entrenchment. Relying on others for validation or self-worth can fortify the ego, wherein relationships are seen as extensions of one's identity rather than genuine connections between individuals.

Healthy relationships foster an environment conducive to spiritual growth by encouraging individuals to confront their insecurities and address their egoic narratives. Communicating openly, practicing empathy, and cultivating vulnerability can disarm the protective layers erected by the ego. As Brene Brown articulates in her work on vulnerability, embracing our imperfections and allowing ourselves to be seen can diminish the power that the ego holds over our interactions.

Conversely, unhealthy attachments can sabotage personal and spiritual development. Co-dependent relationships often entrench individuals within stagnant cycles, perpetuating patterns of neediness and fear. Recognizing this influence underscores the importance of cultivating self-awareness in relational contexts. Acknowledging how we engage with others—and how they reflect our inner landscapes—empowers us to discern whether we are acting from a place of authenticity or manipulating dynamics to serve our ego.

The Lifelong Journey of Awareness

Ultimately, the journey toward transcending the ego is a lifelong endeavor. The spiritual path is characterized by ongoing inquiry, self-reflection, and a persistent willingness to excavate the layers of self-imposed limitations. This journey is neither linear nor consistently pleasing; it is marked by setbacks and revelations that can rattle the individual's foundation. Yet, it is precisely through striving for awareness and allowing ourselves to witness our experience without judgment that we come closer to embodying our truest selves.

Cultivating a daily practice of reflection—whether through journaling, meditation, or simple contemplation—can establish a framework for this ongoing exploration. Such practices can facilitate a deeper understanding of how the ego operates, revealing patterns that may have previously gone unnoticed. Consistent awareness nurtures a sense of groundedness amidst life's unpredictabilities, inviting a greater capacity for presence.

Through this sustained engagement, individuals can reach a significant understanding: that spiritual awakening is not merely an abstract goal but a practical reality. It unfolds in the mundane moments of life—in conversations, in moments of discomfort, in silences broken by laughter. Each instance where one consciously chooses to act from love, compassion, and authenticity rather than fear, contempt, or the weighty expectation of the ego paves the way for a richer, more profound existence.

As the journey deepens, one learns to embrace the ebb and flow of life itself. The acceptance of uncertainty as a natural part of the human experience allows for engagement with the world from a place of openness rather than avoidance. When the ego's need for control lessens, an individual can find strength not in rigid beliefs or identities but in their ability to adapt, grow, and learn throughout life's inevitable transformations.

This exploration of the spiritual path and the egoic construct urges a transformative response that reverberates throughout the existence of every seeker. In recognizing, confronting, and dismantling the layers that separate us from our authentic selves, we embark on the journey home— to a deeper understanding of what it means to be truly alive, connected, and whole.

DUALISTIC CONSTRUCT

Humanity continues to grapple with the profound concepts introduced by Plato in his Allegory of the Cave. The allegory serves as a poignant reflection on the limitations imposed by relying solely on our immediate senses to comprehend the true nature of reality. Even in our modern age, it seems that illusions and shadows more ensnare us than ever before.

Plato, through the voice of Socrates in his work "Republic," paints a vivid picture of a group of individuals who have spent their entire existence chained within the confines of a dark cave. These prisoners are bound to a wall, facing a stark, empty surface. Their only exposure to the external world comes from the shadows cast upon the wall by objects passing in front of a fire behind them. The prisoners, devoid of any other frame of reference, ascribe names and meanings to these fleeting shadows, mistaking them for reality itself.

Socrates expounds on the idea that true enlightenment lies in breaking free from the confines of the cave. The philosopher, akin to a prisoner liberated from his chains, comes to realize the fallacy of mistaking shadows for reality. By venturing outside the cave and witnessing the radiant brilliance of the sun, the philosopher glimpses the true essence of reality that lies beyond the mere illusions projected on the cave wall. The journey from darkness to light symbolizes the transformative power of knowledge and enlightenment.

As the prisoners awaken to the existence of a world beyond their limited perceptions, they are faced with a profound choice. The blinding light of the sun serves as a metaphor for the unveiling of a higher realm of existence, a realm governed by pure Forms and truths that transcend the constraints of the sensory world. However, just as the prisoners in the cave are initially hesitant to embrace this newfound reality, so too are we as human beings often resistant to relinquishing our ingrained beliefs and perceptions in favor of a higher truth.

Plato's Allegory of the Cave is deeply intertwined with the analogy of the sun and the divided line, forming a triad of philosophical insights that illuminate the nature of reality and knowledge. The imprisonment within the cave symbolizes the state of ignorance and confinement that shackles the human mind. At the same time, the journey towards the light represents the pursuit of enlightenment and intellectual liberation.

The freed prisoner's return to the cave serves as a poignant reminder of the challenges inherent in sharing newfound wisdom with those who remain ensnared by shadows. The blindness experienced upon re-entering the cave underscores the dissonance between the enlightened individual and those still trapped within the confines of ignorance. The reluctance of the prisoners to embrace the truth revealed by the returned traveler speaks to the inherent resistance to change ingrained within human nature.

Plato's Allegory of the Cave continues to resonate with audiences across the ages, serving as a timeless parable that challenges us to reexamine our understanding of reality and the pursuit of knowledge. In a world inundated with illusions and shadows, it beckons us to question the validity of our perceptions. It encourages us to seek enlightenment beyond the confines of our self-imposed limitations.

The world beyond the confines of the cave is a reality that many refuse to acknowledge. Trapped in the comfort of the familiar, they cling to the shadows on the wall, content with their limited perception of reality. Yet, the truth lies just outside the entrance, waiting to be discovered. To experience the awakening, one must turn their attention away from the illusions that confine them. It is a painful process, as the eyes struggle to adjust to the intensity of the light, preferring the safety of the darkness. This fear of the unknown drives many back into the recesses of their self-imposed prisons, clinging to the shadows of their ignorance. Shedding the old skin, as snakes do, is a challenging and unfamiliar process. It requires a considerable investment of time, energy, and resolve to adapt to the new paradigm. But for those who are willing to venture forth, the rewards are immense. The world beyond the cave is a revelation, a realm of truth and possibility that transcends the limitations of their previous existence. The path to enlightenment is not an easy one, but it is a journey worth undertaking. It is the only way to discover the true nature of oneself and the world that lies beyond the confines of the cave.

As humanity strives to transcend the shadows of ignorance and embrace the brilliance of truth, we are reminded of the enduring power of philosophical inquiry and the unending quest for enlightenment that defines the human experience. Plato's Allegory of the Cave stands as a testament to the transformative potential of knowledge and the inherent capacity within each of us to break free from the chains of ignorance and embrace the radiant light of truth.

The people of today, modern humanity, can be likened to those who have lived their entire lives seeing only the shadows on the wall. These shadows represent our thoughts, our self-perceptions, which create the world we believe to be real. However, beyond this realm of thinking lies another world, beyond the confines of our dualistic minds.

The term 'dualism' has been used in various contexts throughout the history of thought. In general, it refers to the idea that within a specific domain, there exist two fundamental kinds or categories of things or principles. For instance, in theology, a dualist is someone who believes in the independent and somewhat equal existence of Good and Evil, or God and the Devil, as forces in the world. Dualism stands in contrast to monism, which posits that there is only one fundamental kind or category of thing or principle, and to pluralism, which asserts the existence of multiple kinds or categories.

Within the realm of philosophy of mind, dualism proposes that the mental and the physical, or mind and body, are fundamentally different in some sense. While common sense dictates the existence of physical bodies and urges the development of a unified worldview, materialist monism often serves as the default perspective. Discussions around dualism typically begin with the acknowledgment of the reality of the physical world and then delve into arguments as to why the mind should not be simply regarded as a component of that world.

Engaging with the complexities of dualism invites us to question the nature of reality and the essence of our existence. When we contemplate the dualistic nature of mind and body, we are compelled to ponder the intricate interplay between our thoughts and the tangible world surrounding us. Is the mind merely an extension of the physical body, or does it possess a distinct essence that transcends the confines of our material being?

Descartes, a prominent figure in the realm of philosophy, famously proposed a form of dualism known as Cartesian dualism. He posited that the mind and body are separate entities, with the mind existing independently of the physical realm. This philosophical perspective gave rise to the notion of the "mind-body problem," a perennial inquiry into the relationship between consciousness and corporeality.

As we navigate the labyrinthine depths of dualistic thought, we are met with profound questions that challenge our perceptions of reality and selfhood. Are we merely products of our physical bodies, or do we possess an intrinsic essence that extends beyond the material realm? The enigma of dualism beckons us to explore the boundaries of our understanding and contemplate the mysteries that lie at the intersection of mind and matter.

In our quest for enlightenment, let us embrace the duality that defines our existence and seek to unravel the mysteries that dwell within the recesses of our consciousness, for it is through the exploration of dualism that we may uncover the truths that illuminate the path to self-discovery and philosophical enlightenment.

In the midst of the cave's shadows lies a hidden truth, just beyond the reach of those who remain stagnant in their perceptions. Despite the alluring existence of another world waiting outside, many choose to cling to the familiarity of the known rather than embrace the uncertainty of the unknown. To awaken to the reality of this alternate realm, one must divert their gaze away from the deceptive shadows cast upon the walls and gaze into the abyss of darkness to witness the glimmer of light beckoning from beyond the cave's entrance.

For those accustomed to the comfort of darkness and the illusions it weaves, the transition to welcoming the light can be a painful metamorphosis. The discomfort of adjusting to the intensity of the truth often drives individuals back into the confines of their caves, where ignorance reigns supreme and shadows dance freely. To embrace this awakening requires a monumental commitment of time, energy, and unwavering determination, for shedding the layers of falsehood and embracing a new paradigm demands courage and perseverance.

Just as snakes shed their old skins to make way for growth, so too must we shed our preconceived notions and beliefs to evolve spiritually. The process of this transformation is gradual and unfamiliar, making acceptance a fragile vulnerability - our own Achilles' heel. To truly break free from the confines of ignorance and revel in the light of truth, we must be willing to leave behind the shadows on the wall, venture into the unknown at the cave's entrance, and discover the profound revelations awaiting on the other side.

We often struggle to let go of the familiar, comfortable ways of living, even when we know they no longer serve us. This resistance to change can leave us feeling lost and vulnerable as we navigate through challenges like declining health, relationship issues, and financial troubles. It's as if our entire world has been turned upside down in these moments of upheaval.

It is necessary to view these difficult times as a required shedding of our old, weak ways to make room for growth and renewal. It's like a process of molting, orchestrated by a higher power to help us evolve into stronger, healthier versions of ourselves. Our minds can sometimes feel like traps, locking us into patterns of thinking and behavior that keep us stuck in a cycle of suffering.

But in reality, this mental prison is just an illusion that we have constructed for ourselves. We have become so identified with this false sense of self that we have fallen into a state of ignorance, believing that this limited reality is all there is. As we begin to awaken to the truth of our situation and strive to break free from these self-imposed limitations, the illusion starts to take on a life of its own.

We fight against the illusion as if it were a reality, unwittingly reinforcing its power over us. This perpetual cycle of delusion keeps us locked in a state of slumber, unable to see beyond the confines of our own creation. Awakening from this dream of separateness, rooted in the egoic self, is the key to liberation.

The egoic self is a product of our conditioning, shaped by our experiences, beliefs, and interpretations of the world. It keeps us trapped in a limited perception of reality, disconnected from our true nature. Breaking free from this mental construct involves transcending the incessant chatter of the mind and embracing a deeper understanding of our interconnectedness with all beings.

As we awaken to the illusion of the egoic self and release our attachments to it, we open ourselves up to a more expansive way of being. This journey of self-discovery and liberation requires courage, persistence, and an unwavering commitment to truth. But the rewards of this awakening are immeasurable, leading us towards a state of inner peace, clarity, and boundless love.

A significant characteristic of the egoic mind is its attachment to the physical form and the validation it seeks through external circumstances. This attachment is not just about physical appearances but extends to possessions, achievements, and intangible assets like knowledge, relationships, and social status.

Such attachments create long-standing resentments, as the egoic self often finds itself in a relentless pursuit of protecting and enhancing its image, fearing anything that might challenge or diminish its perceived worth.

Another manifestation of the egoic state is the constant identification with one's thoughts and emotions. Instead of seeing thoughts and feelings as transient states or responses to specific situations, the egoic self views them as concrete aspects of its identity. For instance, if someone feels anger, sadness, or pride, the egoic mind claims these emotions as "I am angry" or "I am proud," solidifying the association between the emotion and the self.

Eckhart Tolle, a renowned spiritual teacher, offers profound insights into the workings of the egoic mind. In his teachings, Tolle describes the egoic mind as a noisy chamber filled with incessant chatter, judgments, and interpretations. This chatter, often grounded in the past or projecting into the future, overshadows the true self, which exists in the present moment. The true self, often called consciousness or awareness, is a state of pure being, untouched by the mind's whims.

Ironically, while the egoic self's search is often for genuine connection, contentment, and peace, its nature leads it astray. By mistaking the false self (egoic self) for the true essence of our being, individuals find themselves trapped in cycles of negative emotions, reactive patterns, and dissatisfaction. The egoic self thrives on division, comparison, and conflict, constantly reinforcing patterns that pull individuals away from the tranquility and clarity of the present moment.

The journey from egoic to non-egoic is a transformative path from illusion to truth, from temporary constructs to eternal presence. It is about recognizing the transient nature of thoughts and emotions and rediscovering the boundless essence beneath the mental noise.

As we continue along the path of awakening to the illusion of the egoic self, a profound shift occurs within us, propelling us towards a more expansive way of existing. This journey of self-discovery demands unwavering courage and a deep commitment to uncovering the truth that lies beyond the veils of the ego.

The ego's grip on the physical form and its ceaseless craving for external validation bind us to a limited perception of reality. It clings not only to appearances but also to material possessions, achievements, and intangible elements like relationships and social standing.

These attachments weave a web of resentment and fear, as the egoic self tirelessly labors to safeguard its constructed identity from any potential threats to its perceived importance. The ego's stronghold lies in the illusion that external factors define our worth.

Moreover, the ego traps us in a constant identification with our thoughts and emotions, blurring the line between transient mental states and our true essence. It narrates a story in which emotions like anger, sadness, or pride are mistaken as integral parts of our identity, reinforcing the illusion of the egoic self.

Eckhart Tolle's wisdom sheds light on the cacophony of the egoic mind, a realm filled with incessant noise, judgments, and projections that obscure our connection to the present moment. Amidst the chaos of the ego's chatter, the essence of our being, pure consciousness or awareness, remains untouched and undisturbed.

Paradoxically, while the egoic self yearns for authentic connection and inner peace, its very nature leads us astray. By misidentifying the egoic self as our true nature, we inadvertently immerse ourselves in a cycle of discontent, reactive behavior, and perpetual dissatisfaction. The ego thrives on separation, comparison, and discord, pulling us further away from the serenity and clarity of the eternal now.

The transition from the egoic state to a non-egoic existence marks a profound transformation from illusion to truth, from ephemeral constructs to eternal presence. It entails a deep understanding of the impermanent nature of thoughts and emotions, guiding us toward rediscovering the boundless essence that lies beneath the turbulent waters of the mind.

As we delve deeper into the realm of awakened consciousness, shedding the layers of the egoic self, we embark on a profound journey towards true liberation and self-realization. This path requires steadfast courage, unwavering commitment, and a relentless pursuit of inner truth. The riches that await us on this transformative expedition are beyond measure, guiding us toward a state of profound serenity, crystal-clear clarity, and limitless love.

One of the core aspects of the egoic mind is its insatiable thirst for validation through external sources, whether physical appearance, material possessions, accolades, or intangible attributes like social standing and knowledge. These attachments not only breed deep-seated resentments but also compel the egoic self into a perpetual quest to safeguard and bolster its perceived worth, fearing any threat to its fragile facade.

Furthermore, the egoic state is characterized by a continuous identification with thoughts and emotions, mistaking them as integral components of one's identity rather than passing states or reactions to external stimuli. When experiencing emotions like anger, sadness, or pride, the egoic mind binds these fleeting feelings with the core essence, proclaiming, "I am angry" or "I am proud," thus reinforcing the illusion of emotional entrapment.

Renowned spiritual luminary Eckhart Tolle illuminates the labyrinthine workings of the egoic mind with profound clarity. Tolle paints a vivid picture of the ego as a cacophonous chamber brimming with ceaseless chatter, judgments, and interpretations, concealing the pure essence of the true self existing in the eternal now. This true self, often referred to as consciousness or awareness, stands untarnished by the caprices of the mind.

Paradoxically, while the egoic self yearns for genuine connection, inner peace, and fulfillment, its very nature steers it off course. By misidentifying the false self (egoic self) as the authentic core of our being, individuals become ensnared in a maze of negative emotions, reactive behaviors, and perennial discontent. Fueled by division, comparison, and strife, the egoic self perpetuates cycles that estrange individuals from the tranquil sanctuary of the present moment.

The transition from the egoic state to the realm of non-egoic existence symbolizes a profound metamorphosis from illusion to truth, from ephemeral constructs to timeless presence. It entails acknowledging the impermanent nature of thoughts and emotions, unveiling the boundless essence that resides beneath the veil of mental cacophony.

The process of awakening involves moving away from our identification with the concept of "me" or "I." Despite our efforts, true freedom seems elusive as our internal prison accompanies us wherever we go. Awakening does not entail overpowering the mind or escaping the confines of the "matrix." Rather, by disassociating from these constructs, we can embrace reality fully, without being consumed by desires or fears.

A BUDDHIST PERSPECTIVE

To grasp the idea of penetrating reality's fabric, one must delve into Buddhism's insightful perspective. Buddhism defines this as the ability to perceive the fundamental essence of phenomena. Yet, a question arises: What reality lies within seemingly empty phenomena? To solve this puzzle, one must explore Buddhism's core principle of śūnyatā, emptiness. Unlike common beliefs equating emptiness with nothingness, śūnyatā actually entails a profound understanding of the relative nature of existence. It serves as a key concept that prevents any phenomenon from attaining true self-existence or substantiality.

In Buddhist teachings, a phenomenon is considered śūnya because it lacks an inherent self, mainly due to its state of relative or dependent origination, known as paticca-samuppada. This doctrine emphasizes the absence of an intrinsic or transcendent self in any entity. Instead, an entity's existence is constantly dependent on external factors and conditions. Therefore, everything perceived or understood inherently carries the mark of what it is not.

Embarking on the journey of unraveling the depths of reality through the lens of Buddhism requires a keen exploration of the concept of emptiness. Within the intricate tapestry of Buddhist philosophy, the essence of phenomena is not viewed through a superficial lens but rather perceived with an eye for the profound. What unfolds before us is a philosophical inquiry into the very nature of existence itself.

Emptiness, or śūnyatā, stands as a cornerstone in the realms of Buddhist wisdom. It is not a mere void or absence but, in fact, a gateway to understanding the inherent relational nature of all things. This concept challenges conventional notions of substantiality by revealing the ever-evolving interplay of causes and conditions that shape our perception of reality.

Central to Buddhist thought is the principle of dependent origination, paticca-samuppada, which illuminates the interconnectedness of all phenomena. By acknowledging the absence of an intrinsic self within any entity, Buddhism unveils the illusion of autonomous existence. Instead, each entity is a product of innumerable external influences, constantly mirroring the essence of what it is not.

In the intricate web of existence, every perception, every understanding carries within it the imprint of its contingent nature. To grasp the essence of reality, one must embrace the fluidity of existence and transcend the illusion of inherent selfhood. Thus, the profound teachings of Buddhism shed light on the boundless depths of emptiness, guiding us toward a more nuanced understanding of the world around us.

Fabric of Reality

The essence of a phenomenon is intricately linked to the ever-changing nature of the phenomena on which it depends. In Buddhism, understanding the fabric of reality involves grasping the ephemeral quality of phenomena, interconnected with each other. True insight into the nature of the world is achieved by recognizing the absence of inherent reality in all things, as they are intertwined with other entities.

Central to Buddhism is the principle of paticca-samuppada, highlighting the interdependent arising of phenomena, which leads to their intrinsic emptiness. This realization acts as a key to liberating individuals from attachment to essentialism and the idea of a permanent self, unveiling the transitory nature of the phenomenal world and freeing them from mundane suffering.

According to Buddhism, human suffering often stems from clinging to the perceived permanence of entities, including the self. Suffering arises when individuals mistakenly believe in the fixed nature of objects and concepts. Enlightened beings, on the other hand, comprehend the interconnectedness present in every phenomenon, transcending such suffering by understanding the continuous formation of the self without any rigid identity.

In Buddhist philosophy, the concept of the self is fluid, lacking inherent existence and relying on external influences. Buddhism encourages letting go of attachment to the material world, emphasizing that true insight into existence can only be attained by freeing oneself from such attachments.

Delving deeper into the essence of Buddhist teachings reveals the profound wisdom embedded within the exploration of impermanence and interconnectedness. The core philosophy revolves around unraveling the illusion of solidity in the fabric of reality, urging individuals to embrace the fluidity of existence.

Through the practice of mindfulness and self-reflection, followers of Buddhism cultivate a heightened awareness of the transient nature of all phenomena. By recognizing the interdependent nature of existence, they come to realize that true liberation lies in letting go of fixed perceptions and embracing the ever-evolving flow of life.

At the heart of Buddhist contemplation lies the fundamental truth that the self is a construct, constantly shaped by external influences and devoid of intrinsic essence. This profound insight shatters the illusion of a separate, unchanging identity, paving the way for individuals to break free from the shackles of ego and attachment.

The teachings emphasize the impermanence of all things, urging practitioners to release their grip on material attachments and the illusions of permanence. By understanding the dynamic interplay of causes and conditions that give rise to phenomena, one can transcend the cycle of suffering and awaken to the interconnected web of existence.

In essence, the journey towards enlightenment in Buddhism is a profound exploration of the intricate dance of impermanence and interconnectedness. It is through embracing the fluidity of existence and relinquishing the illusion of a fixed self that individuals can experience true freedom and discover the boundless potential of their interconnected being.

The inherent essence remains eternal and constant, existing in the eternal present. The state of enlightenment signifies the fusion with the original spiral of existence.

The ancient Pythagorean philosopher Plato once cryptically suggested the existence of a golden key that unlocks the mysteries of the universe. This golden key, referred to as the intelligence of the logos or the primordial OM, is essentially the mind of God. Our human senses can only perceive the outer manifestations of the intricate self-similar mechanics that lie beneath the surface of reality. The source of this divine symmetry remains the most profound mystery of our existence.

Throughout history, great thinkers like Pythagoras, Kepler, Leonardo da Vinci, Tesla, and Einstein have all encountered this mysterious threshold of understanding. Einstein himself described the experience of encountering the mysterious as the most beautiful thing one can come across. This sense of wonder and awe in the face of the unknown is what distinguishes a truly alive individual from one who remains closed off from such experiences.

In a way, we are all like children entering a vast library filled with books in languages we do not yet comprehend. We recognize that these books must have authors, but we struggle to grasp the intricacies of how they were written. There seems to be an underlying order in the arrangement of these books, hinting at a deeper meaning that eludes our understanding. This feeling of awe and recognition of a higher power at work in the universe is a common experience shared by both scientists delving into the mysteries of the cosmos and mystics exploring the depths of their own consciousness.

Ultimately, every profound inquiry into the nature of reality leads to the discovery of the Primordial Spiral, an ancient and enigmatic symbol that represents the interconnectedness of all things and the underlying order that governs the universe. Through science and introspection, we come to realize that this grand tapestry of existence is woven with threads of mystery and beauty, inviting us to contemplate the unfathomable depths of creation.

As we journey further into the realms of the unknown, the whispers of ancient wisdom guide us towards the elusive golden key that unlocks the enigmatic mysteries of the universe. Plato's cryptic allusions to the intelligence of the Logos or the primordial OM beckon us to delve deeper into the mind of God, transcending our limited human senses to grasp the intricate symmetries that underpin reality itself. The veils of illusion begin to lift, revealing a world pulsating with unseen energies and hidden connections.

Through the annals of time, visionaries such as Pythagoras, Kepler, da Vinci, Tesla, and Einstein have gazed upon this cosmic threshold, their souls stirred by the ineffable beauty of the unknown. Like intrepid explorers in a vast library of existence, we stand in awe of the intricate tapestry around us, sensing the presence of an unseen hand guiding the dance of creation. The arrangement of the cosmic books whispers secrets of a divine order waiting to be deciphered by those willing to dive deep into the mysteries of existence.

In the silence of contemplation, the Primordial Spiral emerges as a timeless symbol of interconnectedness, weaving together the fabric of all things in a cosmic dance of harmony. Both scientists probing the depths of the cosmos and mystics plumbing the depths of their own consciousness find themselves drawn to this symbol, recognizing it as a testament to the unity that underlies all diversity. With each revelation, we are invited to cast aside the veil of ignorance and embrace the profound beauty and wonder that permeates the very essence of creation.

A millennium before the construction of Stonehenge, the spiral reigned as a ubiquitous symbol on Earth. Ancient spirals, reflecting growth, expansion, and cosmic energy in the sun and heavens, were prevalent across the globe. From Europe to North America, New Mexico to China, these spirals appeared in various indigenous cultures, signifying the source of energy—the Primordial Mother—in native traditions. Dating back five thousand years, the Neolithic spirals in Newgrange, Ireland, predate the Great Pyramid at Giza by five hundred years, baffling modern observers with their enigmatic nature.

The spiral harks back to an era when humanity felt deeply connected to the Earth, attuned to the natural cycles and rhythms, and less absorbed by mere thoughts. It represents what we perceive as the torque of the universe, where Prana or creative force intertwines with Akasha, shaping a continuum of solid forms. Manifesting between the macrocosm and the microcosm, spiral patterns can be observed in everything from spiral galaxies to DNA, embodying the direct experience of one's energy.

Spirals and helices abound in nature, seen in phenomena like snail shells, sea coral, spider webs, fossils, and seahorses' tails. These natural spirals often follow logarithmic or growth patterns, where sections expand in significance as you move outward from the center. Similar to Indra's Net of Jewels, these spirals exhibit self-similar or holographic characteristics, with each part reflecting the whole in a harmonious dance of patterns.

Two and a half millennia ago, Plato in ancient Greece revered continuous geometric proportion as the most profound cosmic bond, with the Golden Ratio standing as nature's most treasured secret. This divine proportion, expressed through the ratio of A + B to A equaling A to B, symbolizes the world's soul resonating in harmonic unity. The same pentagonal pattern seen in nature, from starfish to the planet Venus's orbital path, bridges the intelligible forms of the heavens above with the material objects of the visible world below. Logarithmic spiral patterns, pervasive and archetypal, echo throughout creation, from the Romanesco broccoli to the arms of galaxies, with our very own Milky Way featuring multiple spiral arms bearing the same logarithmic symmetry.

The pitch of a spiral determines the tightness of its turns, like a plant swaying in the life spiral's rhythm in a time-lapse video. A golden spiral, growing outward by the Golden Ratio factor, mirrors a special mathematical relationship recurrent in nature's design. This observable pattern follows the Fibonacci series, where each number unfolds as the sum of its preceding two. Kepler uncovered self-similar spiral patterns like leaf arrangements on plants and flower petals, highlighting the pervasive presence of such patterns across nature's canvas.

From the spacing of leaves to the phyllotaxis arrangements in plants and DNA structures, self-organizing patterns abound, shaping everything from family trees to pinecones and snowflakes. Nature effortlessly weaves these geometries, repeating them across diverse scales without the need for calculation. Precise and efficient, nature adheres to these patterns in building structures, maximizing exposure to light and nutrients and even aiding predators in their efficient hunting strategies.

The ability to perceive the spiral of life infusing Akasha into material form correlates with appreciating beauty and symmetry in nature, as poet William Blake eloquently expressed. While the study of natural patterns might be less prevalent in the Western world, ancient China recognized this science as "Li," embodying the dynamic order and patterns woven into all living entities. The intricate network of patterns, like branching structures observable at all scales, reflects a fundamental order ingrained in nature, resonating from leaves' arteries to the veined patterns on rocks.

Branching patterns, exemplified in images like the "millennium run" simulation of dark matter distribution, reveal the universe as a vast interconnected web akin to a giant brain. This invisible network of dark matter pulses with unfathomable energy, propelling the universe's expansion and growth. Nature mirrors this branching complexity in structures like tree-like crystals grown with electricity, showcasing the self-organizing beauty inherent in natural processes.

Johann Wolfgang Von Goethe's words underscore the intricate beauty emanating from nature's hidden laws, hinting at a world teeming with self-organizing vitality. The observation of fractal branching, mirrored in the human body's intricate systems like energy meridians, points to a deeper understanding of body functions beyond conventional Western medicine. Energy meridians akin to tree structures, such as the nadis in Eastern medical practices, remain vital channels for energy flow and holistic well-being, their existence transcending physical examination and requiring a deeper internal observation.

Cultivating equanimity through meditation creates a state of nonresistance in the body, facilitating the flow of Prana or inner energy through the nadis and chakras. By focusing attention inward and reducing resistance to bodily sensations, individuals can enhance their energetic capacity and establish vibrant connections within themselves. The alignment of consciousness with these energy pathways leads to a blossoming of physical and energetic connections, establishing intricate wiring patterns akin to those observed in the natural world.

In essence, the interplay of energy flow and physical wiring patterns within the body mirrors the inherent beauty and order found in nature's self-organizing principles. By harmonizing consciousness with the internal energy systems, individuals can unlock profound pathways to vitality and well-being, resonating with the pulsating rhythms of the universe's interconnected web of life.

As we stand on the threshold of the unknown, the ancient wisdom of the universe beckons to us with its enigmatic beauty and profound mysteries. From the cosmic depths to the intricate patterns of existence woven into our very being, the Primordial Spiral whispers to our souls, connecting us to the timeless dance of creation. This symbol of interconnectedness, resonating through the fabric of reality, invites us to delve deeper into the secrets of existence and embrace the harmony that lies at the heart of all things.

The spirals that manifest in nature, from the shells of snails to the arms of galaxies, carry within them the essence of growth, evolution, and cosmic energy. These patterns, echoing the divine proportions of the Golden Ratio, reveal a fundamental order that transcends the visible world, bridging the gap between the heavens above and the tangible world below. Just as Plato revered the cosmic bond of geometric proportion, we, too, can witness the intricate symmetries of nature unfolding in a harmonious dance of patterns that mirror the very soul of the world.

Kepler's insights into the self-similar spiral patterns that adorn the natural world highlight the pervasive presence of ancient geometries that shape our reality. From the Fibonacci series to the logarithmic spirals that define the growth of plants and flowers, nature effortlessly weaves these patterns across diverse scales, creating structures that maximize efficiency and beauty. As we observe the branching patterns that intertwine throughout creation, we glimpse the interconnected web of life, resonating with the pulsating vitality of the universe itself.

In the silent contemplation of these patterns, we come to understand the profound harmony that underlies all things, from the veins of a leaf to the dark matter distribution in the cosmos. Through the cultivation of equanimity and introspection, we align our consciousness with the energy pathways that course through our bodies, unlocking vibrant connections and pathways to wellness. Like the intricate wiring patterns found in nature, our internal energy systems reflect the inherent beauty and order that permeates the universe, guiding us towards a deeper resonance with the web of life that binds us all.

In Taoism, the yin-yang symbol serves as a representation of the intertwining spiral forces of nature. It embodies a concept that is neither two nor one, capturing the essence of duality and interconnectedness. Within this ancient philosophy lies the notion of "Hara," symbolized by a yin-yang or spiral swirl, serving as the power center situated in the abdomen below the navel. Hara, translating to sea or ocean of energy, is referred to as the lower dantien in Chinese teachings.

Across various Asian martial arts disciplines, possessing a strong Hara is believed to render a warrior invincible. In the Samurai tradition, a form of ritual suicide known as hara-kiri - often mispronounced as "hairy carry" - involves impaling one's Hara to sever the chi or energy channel. Movement stemming from this core engenders the grounded, fluid motions observed in martial artists, skilled golfers, belly dancers, and Sufi whirling dervishes.

Developing a focused and disciplined consciousness embodies the essence of Hara, akin to finding tranquility amidst chaos. It signifies an intuitive connection to one's energy source, allowing for a deep-rooted alignment with the Earth and the interconnected wisdom shared among all beings. The practice of thinking from the belly, encapsulated by the phrase "hara de kanganasaii," enables individuals to access their inner wisdom and intuition.

In the ancient teachings of Taoism, the yin-yang symbol serves as a reflection of the intricate dance of natural forces. It encapsulates the idea of duality and unity, illustrating the interwoven nature of existence. Central to this philosophy is the concept of "Hara," depicted as a yin-yang or spiral swirl, residing as the core energy center located in the lower abdomen beneath the navel. Hara, meaning the "sea" or "ocean of energy," corresponds to the lower dantian in the realm of Chinese wisdom.

In the realm of diverse Asian martial arts traditions, possessing a potent Hara is believed to equip a warrior with an unbeatable prowess. Within the realm of the Samurai code, a solemn act of self-sacrifice known as hara-kiri - often mispronounced as "hairy carry" - involves piercing one's Hara to sever the chi or energy flow. The movements that emanate from this core serve as the foundation for the poised, flowing actions witnessed in martial artists, adept golfers, belly dancers, and Sufi whirling dervishes.

Cultivating a mindful and disciplined awareness embodies the essence of Hara, akin to discovering serenity amidst tumultuous surroundings. It signifies an intuitive bond with one's wellspring of energy, fostering a profound connection with the Earth and the shared wisdom that unites all living beings. Embracing the practice of gut-centered thinking, encapsulated in the phrase "hara de kanganasaii," empowers individuals to tap into their inner guidance and instinctual knowing with clarity and purpose.

The ancient Australian Aborigines focused on an area just below the navel, where the cord of the rainbow serpent lay coiled. This spot, known as the Hara, symbolizes the evolutionary energy present in humankind. Within the Hara resides the enteric nervous system, often referred to as the "gut-brain," which possesses a complex network of connections like the brain in the head, complete with neurons and neurotransmitters. Operating independently, the gut-brain exhibits its form of intelligence. It serves as a fractal version of the head brain and vice versa.

In the natural world, a healthy bear with a strong heart demonstrates a deep connection to its environment by following the flow of chi through its senses, centered in the Hara or belly. This connection to the dream lodge, a place in native traditions where all knowledge originates, represents the bear's link to the life spiral.

Ancient peoples understood the significance of the spiral long before modern science recognized its importance. Bees, for instance, reflect a profound connection to the source as they participate in a symbiotic system that nurtures beauty and diversity. Serving as a bridge between the macrocosm and microcosm, bees operate within a hive mind that unites all through a shared heart. Through their collective dreams, the hive influences the manifestation of reality.

While many creatures in nature move in unison with one spirit and direction, not all benefit other species as bees do. For example, the locust acts solely in its self-interest, devouring everything in its path without regard for balance or harmony. In contrast, humans possess the unique ability to choose their behavior: to act like a bee in harmony with the environment, or like a locust, causing imbalance and destruction.

In our modern world, humans strive to comprehend the spiral through rational thought, forgetting that we have always been interconnected with it. Over-reliance on thought leads to a sense of separateness and limitation, distancing us from the source. Comparatively, ancient cultures less oriented towards thought aligned more directly with the spiral, embodying a deeper connection to their evolutionary potential.

In ancient Indian traditions, Kundalini symbolizes inner energy rising through the spine in a serpent-like or helix-like pattern. Individuals in these cultures aligned themselves with the spiral through practices like Kundalini yoga, balancing the power of evolution with the stillness of consciousness. The interplay between the feminine channel, Ida, representing the moon, and the masculine channel, Pingala, associated with the sun, when in harmony, allows energy to flow along the Sushumna channel, activating the chakras and unlocking one's full potential.

The term "chakra," derived from Sanskrit, signifies energy centers within the body, visualized as spinning wheels. Kundalini embodies the primordial spiral that orchestrates human existence, serving as a pathway between gross material reality and subtle energies. This energy cannot be forced through willpower or effort but requires a nurturing environment akin to tending a flower garden—preparing the conditions and allowing nature to unfold its course.

As Kundalini awakens within an individual, they begin to discern the spiral's presence in all patterns, both within themselves and in the external world. This spiral acts as a conduit between inner and outer realities, illuminating the interconnectedness of all existence.

In the ever-changing manifestation of the world, the lotus unfolds as a symbol of generation and rebirth, signifying the cycles of commencement and dissolution. Padmapani Avalokiteswara, known as 'the Lotus-Bearer', emerges across ages as the supporter of Kalpas. The 'Age of Brahma' witnesses the birth of a creative deity from the universal lotus. When Kali Yuga comes to an end, Brahma will dwell within a lotus, peacefully floating on the waters, absorbing the winds as he enters a deep slumber.

In the realm of cosmic unfolding, the lotus maintains its revered status as a potent symbol of renewal and transformation, embodying the eternal cycle of beginnings and endings. Padmapani Avalokiteswara, also called 'the Lotus-Bearer', strides through the corridors of time as Kalpas's guardian. During the epoch known as the 'Age of Brahma', a divine being emerges from the cosmic lotus, ushering in a new era of creation and growth. As Kali Yuga draws to a close, Brahma, the primordial deity, finds solace within the embrace of a lotus, peacefully resting upon the tranquil waters, gracefully surrendering to the gentle whispers of the wind as he embarks on a profound slumber – the 'Night of Brahma' or Pralaya.

During Pralaya, Vishnu, the amalgamation of the Hindu Trimurti, conceals within the darkness the embryonic lotus of the world. Vishnu's abode in Vaikuntha or Mount Meru symbolizes the navel of the world, portrayed by the lotus – Vishnu's navel serves as a sanctuary during this cosmic period.

As the ages shift and the cosmic dance continues, the lotus remains a focal point of cosmic creation and dissolution. From the depths of the void, the lotus emerges as a symbol of divine emergence and preservation.

In the cosmic ballet, the lotus unfolds its petals, revealing the intricate design of creation. Brahma, the creator deity, awakens from his lotus throne, bringing forth the realms of existence. Within the lotus, the universe is held in delicate balance, each petal a reflection of the countless worlds and dimensions.

As the ages turn and the cycles repeat, Vishnu, the preserver, cradles the embryonic lotus, protecting creation within its sacred petals. In the heart of Vaikuntha, Vishnu's lotus throne stands as a beacon of stability amid the chaos of existence.

The lotus, with its mesmerizing beauty and divine significance, serves as a reminder of the eternal cycle of birth, death, and rebirth. Through its sacred presence, the lotus connects all beings to the cosmic web of existence, weaving a tapestry of unity and harmony across the cosmos.

Within you lies an intricate web of connections, growing like a never-ending, unfolding flower as you detach from the concept of self. You become a living bridge, linking the realms of time and timelessness, traversing the boundaries of existence. Discovering the immanent self marks just the initial step along a new, profound journey.

For many, the path to awakening is filled with cycles of realization and loss, as one delves into meditation multiple times before fully integrating the insights gained into the fabric of everyday life. It is not uncommon to experience profound revelations about the essence of your being during moments of meditation or deep reflection, only to slip back into old patterns, returning to the familiar darkness of ignorance. It is during these instances of forgetfulness that one finds oneself ensnared once again within the confines of their mental constructs.

To recognize the stillness or emptiness that permeates every aspect of existence is to embrace a dance of emptiness, where tranquility intertwines seamlessly with motion. In awakening, the notion of stillness becomes synonymous with movement, revealing that form and emptiness are not opposing forces but rather intricately entwined aspects of the same reality. These truths may seem nonsensical to the rational mind, which inherently thrives on the dichotomy of dualistic thinking.

Embarking on the spiritual journey is akin to unearthing a labyrinth within oneself, where each turn reveals a hidden connection waiting to be illuminated. As you shed the layers of ego and identity, you step onto a path that transcends the limitations of linear time, embracing the eternal now.

The process of awakening unfolds in a series of cycles, each cycle a spiral deeper into the essence of being. Through meditation and introspection, one glimpses the boundless nature of the self, only to grapple with the transient nature of awareness as it slips through the grasp of the conscious mind. The struggle lies not in the initial realization but in the integration of that truth into the tapestry of daily existence.

Within the ebb and flow of awakening, there are moments of clarity where the veil is lifted, and the unity of all things is revealed in its exquisite simplicity. Yet, as quickly as the truth is grasped, the mind's grip loosens, and one finds oneself adrift in the sea of illusion once more. It is in these moments of forgetfulness that the true test of awakening presents itself, beckoning the seeker to return to the wellspring of inner knowing.

To dance with emptiness is to embrace the void within, to move with grace through the formless expanse of existence. Stillness and motion converge in a divine choreography, revealing that the essence of being is both fullness and emptiness, creation and dissolution. This paradox, though confounding to the logical mind, resonates deep within the awakened soul as a symphony of harmonious dissonance, beckoning the seeker ever closer to the heart of truth.

René Descartes, known as the "Father of Modern Philosophy," is revered for his departure from the traditional Scholastic-Aristotelian philosophy of his era and his advocacy for the emerging mechanistic sciences. His assertion, "I think, therefore I am," serves as the cornerstone of Descartes's philosophy, symbolizing the rejection of civilization's reliance on mere illusions. Descartes, like all humans, erred by conflating the essence of "being" with the act of thinking. In the beginning of his renowned treatises, Descartes contended that nearly everything could be subjected to doubt, prompting skepticism towards even the senses and thoughts.

Seeking to unravel the mysteries of the cosmos, Descartes delved deep into the recesses of his mind, challenging the very foundations of knowledge and existence. His relentless pursuit of truth led him to question the authenticity of the world around him, leading to the famous declaration that sparked a revolution in philosophical thought.

As Descartes grappled with the complexities of reality, he embarked on a journey of introspection unlike any other. With each cogent argument and logical deduction, he sought to strip away the layers of illusion that obscured the truth from his grasp. Through skepticism and inquiry, Descartes sought to establish a firm foundation upon which to build his philosophical edifice.

Despite the uncertainties that plagued his quest for certainty, Descartes stood resolute in his pursuit of knowledge. Armed with reason and intellect, he strove to transcend the confines of traditional thought and embrace a new paradigm of understanding. With each ponderous reflection and meticulous analysis, Descartes laid the groundwork for a new era of philosophical inquiry.

In the hallowed halls of academia, Descartes's ideas reverberated like thunder, challenging the prevailing wisdom of his time. Through his radical departure from convention, he charted a new course for future generations of thinkers to follow. Descartes's legacy endures as a testament to the transformative power of critical inquiry and intellectual courage.

Similarly, the Kalamas Sutra is distinguished for promoting free inquiry and embodying teachings free from fanaticism, bigotry, dogmatism, and intolerance. The rationality of the Dhamma, the Buddha's teachings, is notably exemplified by its openness to meticulous scrutiny at every stage of the path to enlightenment. The training for wisdom, culminating in the purity of the arahant, is intricately linked with the examination and analysis of internal phenomena such as sensory perceptions and mental concepts. Insight plays a vital role in correctly comprehending all phenomena in Dhamma, leading to the rejection of detrimental beliefs and the adoption of beneficial ones.

In a similar vein, the Kalamas Sutra serves as a timeless beacon of wisdom, advocating for the questioning of beliefs and the rejection of blind faith. It stands as a testament to the importance of critical thinking and a discerning mind in one's spiritual journey. Just as the Dhamma encourages individuals to question and investigate, the Kalamas Sutra instills the value of intellectual rigor and self-examination.

By nurturing the seeds of inquiry and skepticism, one can navigate the labyrinth of spiritual teachings with clarity and purpose. The Kalamas Sutra, like a guiding compass, directs seekers towards a path free from the shadows of ignorance and deceit. Through its teachings, individuals are empowered to embrace reason and discernment, forging a foundation of understanding built on personal insight and wisdom.

The methods of examination outlined in the Kalamas Sutra underscore the importance of perceiving things as they truly are, aligning with the principles of logical thinking. Critical analysis and evaluation are integral to cultivating wisdom, as true insight cannot emerge suddenly without being influenced by thoughtful contemplation. The process of penetrating and understanding phenomena is indispensable for acquiring a clear vision and fostering intellectual development. Ultimately, the significance of critical thinking in refining one's understanding and attaining profound wisdom cannot be understated.

As an expert in philosophy and logic, I wholeheartedly agree with the teachings of the Kalamas Sutra. Examining things with a critical eye is paramount in gaining a deeper understanding of the world around us. Without questioning and analyzing, we risk falling into ignorance and misunderstanding. True wisdom is not handed to us on a silver platter; it requires diligent observation and contemplation. By honing our critical thinking skills, we pave the way for enlightenment and intellectual growth. Let us continue to embrace this timeless wisdom and engage in thoughtful reflection to uncover the truths that lie beneath the surface.

In a parallel universe where Descartes and the teachings of the Kalamas Sutra intertwined, a profound synergy emerged in the pursuit of truth and enlightenment. Descartes, with his relentless skepticism, found common ground with the Kalamas in questioning the very fabric of reality. As he delved deeper into the realms of doubt, he encountered the Kalamas' philosophy of free inquiry, resonating with their emphasis on critical analysis.

The essence of "being" that Descartes grappled with found a new dimension in the teachings of the Kalamas. The pursuit of wisdom, guided by rational examination, mirrored Descartes' quest for clarity amidst the uncertainty of existence. Both philosophies converged on the profound importance of perceiving reality as it truly is, unfettered by illusions or preconceived notions.

As Descartes honed his powers of critical thinking, he began to see the parallels between his own journey and the path to enlightenment laid out by the Kalamas. The meticulous scrutiny of internal phenomena, the deconstruction of sensory perceptions and mental concepts—all of which echoed Descartes' methodical approach to unraveling the mysteries of the mind.

Through the union of Descartes' methodical doubt and the Kalamas' teachings on insight, a new paradigm of intellectual development emerged. The union of these two philosophies underscored the transformative power of critical thinking in unlocking the deeper truths of the universe. In this harmonious blend of Western rationality and Eastern wisdom, a path towards profound understanding and enlightenment beckoned, transcending the boundaries of time and space.

The Kalama Sutta, an integral component of the Dhamma teachings, serves as a guiding beacon for truth seekers, establishing a framework for discerning truth. Central to this sutra are the four solaces, which shed light on the level of uncertainty permissible in matters beyond conventional understanding. These solaces highlight that virtuous living is not contingent solely on faith in concepts such as rebirth or karmic consequences. Rather, the key emphasis lies in cultivating mental well-being through overcoming desires, aversions, and ignorance. This underscores that the core motivation for leading a moral life stem from attaining inner peace and wisdom by relinquishing greed, hatred, and delusion. The teachings encapsulated within the Kalama Sutta form a cornerstone for individuals navigating the path of enlightenment and self-discovery within the Buddhist tradition.

SELF-REALIZATION AND AWAKENING

On the journey towards self-realization and awakening, the Kalama Sutta serves as a guiding light, offering wisdom and clarity to illuminate the path ahead. By prompting individuals to question, investigate, and discern rather than passively accepting beliefs, this sacred text upholds the importance of critical thinking and personal experience in the pursuit of truth. It underscores ethical conduct not merely as a means to earn favor with a deity, but as a pathway to purify the mind and free oneself from the chains of craving and ignorance.

The concept of the four solaces resonates deeply, providing comfort to those bewildered by the multitude of teachings and doctrines they encounter. By acknowledging the inherent uncertainty in matters beyond immediate perception, the Buddha empowers seekers to rely on their powers of reasoning and introspection. This empowerment enables individuals to cultivate a deeper understanding of themselves and the world, fostering inner resilience and clarity.

Ultimately, the Kalama Sutta stands as a timeless reminder that genuine liberation arises not from blind adherence to dogma, but from the genuine exploration of one's mind and heart. It invites us to embrace the transformative power of wisdom and compassion, guiding us towards a life rooted in integrity, kindness, and profound insight. As we traverse the path of self-discovery, may the teachings of the Kalama Sutta continue to inspire and uplift us on our spiritual journey towards awakening.

Moncure D. Conway's journey to the Wise Men of the East, chronicled in "My Pilgrimage to the Wise Men of the East," took place over fifty years ago in Colombo. Accompanied by Ponnambalam Ramanathan, then Solicitor General of Ceylon, Conway ventured to the Vidyodaya Pirivena to delve into the Buddha's teachings under the tutelage of Hikkaduve Siri Sumangala Nayaka Thera, the venerable founder of the institution. The Nayaka Thera expounded upon the foundational principles of the Kalama Sutta to Conway and Ramanathan during a profound and enlightening dialogue. As they concluded their conversation, Ramanathan whispered to Conway, reflecting on the irony of their shared experience: "Isn't it remarkable that we, originating from diverse faiths and distant lands, have united in pursuit of a sermon from the Buddha advocating for unrestrained contemplation and a commitment to challenging conventional dogmas, the essence of human progress?"

Conway nodded in contemplation, their shared epiphany resonating deeply within him. The peaceful ambiance of the sunlit courtyard at Vidyodaya Pirivena seemed to echo with the timeless wisdom passed down through generations. Ramanathan's words lingered in the air, conveying a universal truth that transcended cultural, religious, and geographical boundaries. As they bid farewell to the venerable Nayaka Thera, a sense of camaraderie enveloped the two men, acknowledging their shared quest for enlightenment beyond traditional confines.

Their pilgrimage to the Wise Men of the East not only broadened their intellectual horizons but also illuminated the intrinsic unity of all truth seekers. Conway and Ramanathan walked together, their hearts brimming with newfound respect for the interconnectedness of humanity's spiritual journey. In that serene moment, amidst the whispers of ancient wisdom carried on the tropical breeze, they recognized that the pursuit of enlightenment knows no bounds or labels—it is a universal endeavor that transcends time and space, embracing all who embark on its sacred path. As they stepped out into the vibrant streets of Colombo, they carried not only the Buddha's teachings but also a profound bond forged in the crucible of shared discovery.

Both the Buddha and Descartes embarked on their philosophical journeys from a place of profound skepticism. They both delved into the concept of "truth," yet their paths diverged in their pursuit of understanding. Descartes chose to halt his inquiry at the realm of thought, while the Buddha delved deeper, penetrating beyond the surface levels of the mind into the realms of consciousness. Had Descartes ventured further beyond mere intellectual contemplation, he may have come to realize his true nature, potentially altering the landscape of Western consciousness significantly.

Instead, Descartes introduced the notion of a malevolent demon capable of ensnaring humanity in a veil of illusion—a conception reminiscent of the premise explored in the film "The Matrix." These cinematic narrative challenges conventional perceptions of reality by proposing that our existence is not inherently real but rather a simulated construct engineered by advanced artificial intelligence. Through this lens, mental states are depicted as potentially reducible to physical manifestations.

It is a fundamental aspect of human nature to attribute external factors to the circumstances of our world and the nature of our reality. Ironically, the malevolent demon that Descartes envisioned can be seen as a metaphor for the self—the construct that defines and limits our perceptions. True awakening reveals the presence of a controller, akin to a machine or evil demon draining our essence day by day. This controller manifests through the persona—the intricate web of subprograms or inner wardens that dictate our desires and impulses.

These wardens relentlessly impel us towards pursuing more—be it in terms of material possessions, status, power, or acclaim—fueling an unquenchable, insatiable thirst within us. The chief warden orchestrates the quest for recognition and prestige, striving to elevate the self above all others. However, these desires are insatiable, prompting us to invest significant effort in adorning our metaphorical prisons and maintaining the facades we present to the world.

The path to true liberation does not lie in succumbing to the dictates of these inner wardens and the self-agenda they propagate. Liberation entails shedding the self-agenda altogether, relinquishing the hold of conditioned patterns and desires. It is a common fear that embracing one's true nature will necessitate sacrificing individuality and the pleasures of worldly existence. Yet, the converse holds true—true individuality can only blossom once the conditioned self is transcended.

By remaining entrenched within our self-constructed caves of illusion, many of us fail to discern the profound messages our souls seek to convey. The journey to awakening necessitates introspection and meditation, allowing us to scrutinize the conditioned self that evolves as we traverse our conscious paths. By arriving at a point of inner stillness—the source of our being—we can attune ourselves to the promptings of the true self without imposing preconceived notions onto our external reality.

In striving to alter our external surroundings to align with our vision of the ideal path, we are akin to individuals attempting to manipulate their reflections in a mirror. True transformation occurs not through manipulating external circumstances, but by realizing and embodying the authentic source behind the reflection. When we awaken to our genuine selves in the mirror, the external world need not fundamentally change; it is our inner energy, freed from conditioned constraints, that becomes receptive to the guidance of the soul. Only by releasing our attachments and cravings for worldly attainments can we unveil the purpose and direction of the soul's journey.

In the realm of philosophy, the Buddha and Descartes stand as beacons of inquiry, navigating the treacherous waters of truth and reality with unwavering determination. Both embarked on their quests fueled by skepticism, seeking to unravel the mysteries that shroud existence.

As Descartes peered into the labyrinth of thought, he glimpsed a malevolent demon casting shadows upon the tapestry of human consciousness. This malevolent force, whether a physical entity or a metaphorical construct, mirrors the insidious nature of the self—ever-present, orchestrating desires that bind us to worldly illusions.

Within the chambers of our minds, the wardens of the self lay in wait, whispering seductive promises of fulfillment through material wealth, status, and power. Yet, these promises remain hollow echoes, echoing the deception woven by the malevolent demon that lurks within.

True liberation beckons from beyond the confines of the self, calling for a shedding of conditioned desires and patterns that ensnare us in a cycle of unfulfilled cravings. It is in relinquishing the self-agenda that the seeds of true individuality are sown, blossoming forth in the fertile soil of inner stillness.

To awaken to the messages of the soul and uncover the purpose of our existence, we must embark on a journey of introspection and meditation. By shedding the illusions that cloud our perceptions and obstruct our inner vision, we open ourselves to the whispers of the true self—guiding us towards a path of authentic transformation.

In the mirror of our consciousness, the true self awaits recognition, free from the constraints of conditioned beliefs and external validations. As we release our attachments and cravings for fleeting worldly attainments, the radiant energy of the soul emerges, illuminating the way forward with clarity and purpose. Only by heeding the call of the soul can we unveil the profound meaning behind our existence and embrace the transformative power of awakening.

In the realm of Greek mythology, the gods cast their judgment upon Sisyphus, the infamous king of Ephyra. Known for his deceitful ways and despotic rule, Sisyphus reveled in the suffering of others, disregarding the sacred bonds of hospitality. His heinous deeds did not escape the notice of the divine beings, who decreed a punishment fitting for his crimes.

For his audacity in outwitting death itself not once but twice, and for his flagrant disregard of moral law, Sisyphus was condemned to an eternal and futile task. The gods ordained that he must laboriously push a colossal boulder up a steep hill, only to witness it cruelly roll back down each time he neared the pinnacle. The cycle was to endure endlessly, a ceaseless torment befitting the magnitude of his transgressions.

And so, Sisyphus toiled ceaselessly under the weight of his burden, his efforts destined to be in vain as the boulder mocked his every advance. The gods had spoken, and the punishment was set in stone, a perpetual reminder of the consequences that befall those who dare to defy the will of the divine.

The renowned French existentialist and Nobel Prize-winning author Albert Camus viewed the plight of Sisyphus as a potent metaphor for the human condition. He pondered the profound question: how do we discover meaning in the sheer absurdity of human existence? Humanity, like Sisyphus, seems destined to labor tirelessly, striving for a future that never truly arrives, only to meet the inevitable end of death. Camus suggested that upon realizing this harsh truth, individuals would face a pivotal choice. They could either spiral into madness if they clung to their narrow ego-driven perspectives, or they could experience a profound awakening and break free from the self-imposed confines of their own making. The outer struggles of life, Camus believed, were merely manifestations of our internal realities, serving as reflections of our deepest fears, desires, and beliefs.

He delved deep into the intricacies of the human psyche, exploring the labyrinthine corridors of thoughts and emotions that shape our perceptions of reality. Camus posited that by embracing the existential absurdity of existence, one could pave the way toward a more authentic and liberated way of being. Instead of seeking external validation or purpose, he urged individuals to cultivate an inner sense of fulfillment and acceptance of the inherent uncertainties that define human life. To Camus, the ultimate act of rebellion against the absurdity of the world was to find joy and meaning in the very act of rebellion itself.

The cosmic joke, the absurdity of the situation, becomes clear when there is a complete failure of the egoic self to awaken to its futile pursuits. In Zen, a saying before enlightenment: chop wood, carry water; after enlightenment, chop wood, carry water. Before enlightenment, one must roll the ball up the hill; after enlightenment, one must roll the ball up the hill. What has changed in this scenario is the inner resistance to what is; the struggle has been dropped, rather, or the one who struggles has been realized to be illusory. The individual will, or the individual mind and the divine will or higher mind now align.

As the veil of illusion lifts, revealing the interplay between the individual will and the greater cosmic will, a sense of peace settles upon the once turbulent waters of the mind. The incessant need to control, to grasp and to manipulate gives way to a surrender, a letting go into the flow of existence. Like a leaf carried by a gentle breeze, the awakened being navigates through the unfolding of life with grace and acceptance. The struggle of the egoic self fades into the background, replaced by a profound understanding of the interconnectedness of all things.

In this new paradigm, actions are no longer driven by a sense of lack or a desperate search for meaning. Rather, they emerge effortlessly from a place of deep alignment with the universal rhythms of creation. The simple tasks of everyday life, once viewed as burdens to be overcome, are now embraced as sacred rituals, each movement a dance in harmony with the cosmic symphony.

Through the lens of enlightenment, the mundane becomes infused with magic, the ordinary suffused with the extraordinary. The sound of a bird's song, the feel of the earth beneath one's feet, the warmth of the sun on the skin – all are experienced with a heightened sense of awareness and gratitude. The awakened soul recognizes that every moment, no matter how seemingly insignificant, carries within it the potential for profound revelation.

And so, the journey continues, with each step a meditation and each breath a prayer. Chop wood, carry water – not as a means to an end, but as a celebration of the eternal now. The ball is rolled up the hill, not out of obligation, but out of love for the very act of rolling. In this enlightened state, effort and ease merge into a seamless tapestry of being, where the distinction between the doer and the deed dissolves, and all that remains is the pure essence of existence itself.

SUMADHI

The arduous path

Sumadhi, originating from ancient Sanskrit teachings, embodies the essence of pure awareness – a state of consciousness that surpasses ordinary thought and perception. Within the realms of meditation and mindfulness, the attainment of Sumadhi is revered as the pinnacle of spiritual evolution and enlightenment. It is believed to usher in internal tranquility, mental clarity, and a profound connection to the universal life force that interweaves through all beings. Those who reach the state of Sumadhi are described to undergo profound realizations, heightened intuitive abilities, and a profound sense of unity with the cosmos.

At its core, Sumadhi epitomizes the ultimate aspiration of spiritual seekers – a state of existence where the boundaries of the self dissolve, and one harmonizes completely with the rhythmic flow of life. It is a state of deep stillness and peace, where the ego dissipates, leaving behind only pristine awareness and a profound sense of unity with all existence. While achieving Sumadhi may demand dedicated practice and steadfast commitment, numerous believe that it remains attainable for all who embark on the journey of self-discovery and inner exploration.

Sumadhi fundamentally entails shedding all internal resistance towards the ever-changing phenomena, without exceptions. True Sumadhi is attained by the individual capable of finding inner peace irrespective of external circumstances. The relinquishment of resistance is not an endorsement of specific outcomes but a means to ensure that inner liberty is independent of external factors. It is crucial to recognize that accepting reality as it unfolds does not imply passivity or complacency. Rather, it enables one to act in alignment with the natural flow of existence, devoid of unconscious impulses. Acting in this manner allows one to harness the full potential of inner energy, facilitating effective and purposeful action.

Many argue that true change and the realization of peace necessitate intensified struggle against perceived adversaries. However, fighting for peace is akin to clamoring for silence – it engenders only what one seeks to avoid. Presently, society is embroiled in wars against numerous facets of existence: terrorism, diseases, hunger, to name a few. Yet, every war waged ultimately represents a battle against ourselves, stemming from a collective delusion. Despite claiming to champion peace and human rights, individuals often perpetuate practices that contradict these ideals. This perpetual contradiction signifies a refusal to acknowledge the hidden aspects that perpetuate suffering and strife. The belief in overcoming adversities such as cancer, hunger, or terrorism through warfare sustains the illusion that systemic change is unnecessary. The crux of transformation lies within the inner realm, where a revolution must first transpire. Only when individuals align with the spiral of life within can external reality harmonize with the universal flow. Until such alignment is achieved, any actions undertaken merely contribute to the existing chaos perpetuated by the mind.

The juxtaposition of war and peace is an intrinsic part of the human experience – they coexist along an unending continuum. One cannot exist devoid of the other, much like light without darkness or up without down. The human inclination to seek light without darkness, fullness without emptiness, or happiness without sorrow engenders further fragmentation of the world. Each solution conceived by the egoic mind arises from the premise of a problem, eventually exacerbating the initial issue. Resistance only serves to perpetuate the undesired, emphasizing the notion that what one resists persists.

In the realm of Sumadhi, the merging of war and peace unfolds as a paradoxical dance within the cosmic symphony. It is within the deep chambers of our consciousness that the battles of external reality find their roots. The dichotomy of war and peace is not a battle to be won or lost but a reflection of the internal landscape seeking equilibrium.

To truly embody the essence of peace, one must confront the shadows of war that lurk within. It is by delving into the depths of our being, acknowledging the fears, insecurities, and conflicts that reside there, that we pave the path towards true harmony. The external conflicts we witness are mere reflections of the unresolved turmoil within each individual soul.

The shift towards peace does not entail avoiding or suppressing the existence of war but embracing it with compassion and understanding. Just as darkness is a canvas for light to shine brighter, war serves as a backdrop against which peace can radiate its brilliance. By acknowledging the interconnected nature of these seemingly opposing forces, we transcend duality and step into the realm of unity.

Sumadhi beckons us to embrace the totality of our experiences, both the turbulent storms and the serene moments. Through this acceptance, we unravel the threads of separation that have woven themselves into the fabric of our existence. In the tapestry of life, war and peace are but contrasting shades that, when woven together, create a masterpiece of profound beauty and complexity.

As we navigate the intricacies of existence, let us remember that the path to peace begins within. By tending to the seeds of discord that reside in our hearts, we nurture the sprouts of harmony that have the potential to bloom into a garden of tranquility. In this garden, the flowers of war and peace sway in harmonious unison, whispering the timeless wisdom of Sumadhi – the union of all that is, was, and ever will be.

Human ingenuity creates new antibiotics, only to find nature getting more cunning as bacteria strengthen. Despite our best efforts in the ongoing fight, the prevalence of cancer is increasing. The number of hungry people in the world is steadily growing. The number of terrorist attacks worldwide continues to rise. What is wrong with our approach?

In the current reality that surrounds us, there exists a striking resonance with the evocative imagery from Gertie's poem about the Sorcerer's Apprentice. Within the confines of an ancient chamber pulsating with waves of crackling energy, the youthful apprentice of the sorcerer stood poised, a staff of enchantment clutched firmly in their grasp. Anticipation gleamed in their eyes as they prepared to wield the dormant power concealed within the mystical artifact. Whispers of age-old incantations swirled around the apprentice, enveloping them in a shroud of mystical protection.

With unwavering focus and a steady hand, the apprentice commenced the intricate process of harnessing the raw energy coursing through the staff, molding it into a tangible and potent force. A radiant beam of iridescent light erupted from the staff, casting an ethereal glow over the chamber and igniting a fervor of exhilaration within the apprentice's heart as the magic responded obediently to their thoughts and desires, bending to their will like an obedient servant.

However, a shadow of unease began to creep into the recesses of the apprentice's mind as the unchecked power surged forth with relentless intensity, teetering dangerously close to spiraling out of control. With a furrowed brow, the apprentice grappled to contain the unruly energy, a fierce struggle unfolding between their will and the volatile magic at play. Beads of sweat glistened upon their brow as they fought fervently to regain dominion over the chaotic forces, a riveting clash between master and magic.

Through sheer determination and a final surge of concentrated effort, the apprentice managed to quell the turbulent energy, restoring a semblance of calm to the chamber as the enchanted staff grew tranquil in their grasp. Gasping for breath, the apprentice comprehended the perilous precipice they had traversed, a profound realization of the inherent dangers interwoven with the manipulation of magic. With newfound reverence for the formidable forces they wielded, the sorcerer's apprentice vowed to tread a path of caution and vigilance, wary of the consuming allure that lurked within the very essence of the power they sought to command.

We have taken hold of a great power, but we do not have the wisdom to wield it. The problem lies in our lack of understanding of the tool we are using— the human mind and its proper role and purpose. The crisis stems from the limited condition of our thinking, feeling, and experiencing life. Rationalism has blinded us to the wisdom of ancient cultures, while egoic thinking has dulled our ability to feel life's depth and sacredness. The numinosity of life and the realization of different levels of consciousness are slipping away from humanity.

In the ancient Egyptian tradition, netters, archetypal forms embodying divine characteristics, were accessible only to those who purified their physical and spiritual selves to contain higher consciousness. The original Netter, known as Thoth or Tahuti, symbolized the essence of all knowledge and wisdom. Depicted as a scribe with the head of an Ibis, Thoth represented the cosmic principle of thought, encompassing language, concepts, mathematics, and artistic expressions. Access to Thoth's wisdom required specialized training, as it resided in the Akashic or etheric realm, not confined to a physical book.

Legend spoke of a hidden source of false knowledge shielded by a golden serpent within each human being, echoing the universal myth of a guardian serpent protecting the invaluable treasure. Known by various names such as Kundalini Shakti, Chi, or the Holy Spirit, the serpent symbolized the egoic construct entangled with inner energies that needed to be transcended to attain true wisdom. The Book of Thoth, although promising access to divine secrets and celestial truths, also brought suffering to those who sought to control its power through their ego.

In Egyptian mythology, Osiris personified awakened consciousness, essential for safely navigating the vast realms of knowledge and understanding. Without this awakened state, any knowledge acquired by the limited self could lead to perilous outcomes, severing the connection to higher wisdom. The Eye of Horus, a symbol of clear perception and spiritual insight, needed to be open to navigate the complexities of accessing sacred knowledge.

The narrative alluded to parallels with the story of the fall in the Garden of Eden, where the consumption of the fruit from the Tree of Knowledge of Good and Evil led to humanity's expulsion from paradise. Similarly, humanity had delved into the forbidden knowledge contained within the Book of Thoth, facing the repercussions of seeking divine wisdom without the requisite spiritual preparedness. This cautionary tale reinforced the notion that true enlightenment required more than mere intellectual curiosity; it demanded humility, spiritual attunement, and a harmonious integration of higher principles into one's being.

The serpent, often portrayed as a symbol of the primordial spiral reaching from the microcosm to the macrocosm, is likened to the egoic mind manifested in the tangible world. In contemporary times, the serpent symbolizes the individual - embodying the inner conflict between ego and self. Despite the unprecedented access to vast knowledge and groundbreaking discoveries in the material realm, humanity paradoxically finds itself more constrained and ignorant about its own identity and purpose, leading to a perplexing cycle of suffering. Our thoughts, ingrained with dualistic labels of good or bad, perpetuate a divisive ego structure rooted in self-interest and preference. Escaping this cycle doesn't involve waging wars for peace or attempting to dominate nature but rather an acknowledgment of the underlying truth.

The very existence of the ego fosters a sense of duality, creating artificial boundaries between self and other, mine and yours, man and nature. This fragmentation perpetuates violence, as the ego necessitates separation from others to find its identity. In the absence of the ego, conflict dissipates, hubris diminishes, and the exploitation of nature for personal gain ceases. The current crises plaguing our world mirror an inherent inner turmoil stemming from our profound disconnect with our true essence. Entrapped in egoic constructs defined by race, religion, nationality, and political ideology, we remain entrenched in fear and estranged from our authentic selves. Cohorts and affiliations further reinforce our egoic identities as groups assert their perspectives as the ultimate truth, perpetuating a cycle akin to individual ego battles.

In the present day, Earth is experiencing a multitude of varied realities and firmly held belief systems, leading to contradictory understandings and emotional reactions to common occurrences.

Similarly, samsara and Nirvana coexist within the same realm in Hell, representing two distinct dimensions. What may seem catastrophic to one individual could be viewed as a fortunate occurrence by another. It is becoming increasingly evident that external situations do not necessarily dictate the state of one's inner world.

In the depths of Hell, amidst the chaos and despair, there lies a profound duality between samsara and Nirvana. For some lost souls, the constant cycle of suffering and rebirth symbolizes their eternal plight. Yet, for a select few enlightened beings, Nirvana provides a sanctuary of peace and enlightenment, a realm untainted by the darkness that envelops Hell.

To witness these contrasting dimensions existing side by side is a reminder that perspective is a powerful force. What one deems as a calamity, another might see as a blessing in disguise. The stark difference in how individuals perceive their realities within the same realm highlights the intricate complexity of the human experience.

It serves as a poignant reminder that despite the external turmoil and torment, one's inner world remains a sanctuary that can be shaped and nurtured independently of external circumstances. In the midst of Hell's unending trials, the coexistence of samsara and Nirvana serves as a testament to the resilience of the human spirit and the boundless potential for transformation within even the darkest of realms.

As the flames of adversity licked at their very essence, a glimmer of hope arose from the depths of despair. The juxtaposition of suffering and serenity painted a striking portrait of duality within the human experience. In the heart of chaos, a silent revolution unfolded, empowering souls to transcend the limitations of their physical reality and embrace the infinite possibilities that lay dormant within. Through the crucible of existence, the alchemy of the soul unfolded, forging diamonds of wisdom and compassion from the raw ore of suffering.

Delving into the intricacies of Sumadhi allows us to harmonize with the challenges and hardships that define our reality. It entails reflecting on the journey that paves the way toward attaining samadhi in our everyday lives. Embracing Sumadhi means transforming into a self-sustaining force, propelling us forward on our spiritual path. To realize Sumadhi is to become a self-propelled wheel. To achieve such a state of existence requires unwavering dedication and a deep understanding of the self. The journey towards realizing samadhi is not for the faint-hearted; it demands inner strength and a willingness to confront one's deepest fears and desires. It is a path fraught with obstacles and challenges, but those who persevere will find themselves transformed in ways they never thought possible.

As we embark on this quest for enlightenment, we must be prepared to let go of our attachments and relinquish our ego. Only by shedding the layers of illusion that cloud our vision can we truly connect with the universal consciousness that underlies all of existence. In the stillness of the mind and the purity of the heart, we will discover the boundless joy and serenity that come with the realization of samadhi.

So, let us tread this path with courage and humility, knowing that the ultimate prize is not material wealth or success, but a profound sense of inner peace and unity with the cosmos. May we be guided by the wisdom of ancient sages and the light of our inner knowing as we journey towards the summit of self-realization. The wheel of samadhi awaits, ready to carry us beyond the confines of our limited selves into the vast expanse of universal consciousness.

"To Realize Sumadhi is to Become a Self-Propelled Wheel"

As the ancient monk uttered those profound words, a wave of silence enveloped the dimly lit room. The flickering candlelight cast dancing shadows on the timeworn walls, adding an air of mystique to the moment. Those gathered around him leaned in, their eyes filled with a mix of reverence and curiosity.

"To realize samadhi is to become a self-propelled wheel," he repeated, his voice soft yet commanding. The words seemed to hang in the air, lingering long after they had been spoken. For those who understood the significance of his teachings, it was a moment of clarity, a beacon of enlightenment in a world shrouded in darkness.

In that hushed space, minds expanded, and souls soared. The concept of samadhi, the state of ultimate bliss and oneness with the universe, beckoned to them like a distant but attainable dream. Each individual present felt a stirring within, a profound yearning to unravel the mysteries of existence and grasp the true nature of reality.

And so, they listened, with rapt attention and open hearts, as the monk delved deeper into the essence of samadhi. His words wove a tapestry of wisdom and insight, guiding them on a path of inner exploration and self-discovery. As the night wore on, the boundaries between the physical and the metaphysical blurred, and it seemed as though they were on the cusp of a great revelation.

"To become a self-propelled wheel is to transcend the limitations of the mundane world," the monk intoned, his eyes alight with an otherworldly glow. "It is to harness the power within and propel oneself towards the divine."

And in that moment, a spark ignited within each person present, a spark that would grow into a blazing fire of spiritual awakening. The journey towards samadhi had begun, a journey of self-realization and transcendence that would lead them to the very pinnacle of enlightenment. And as they left the hallowed space that night, each carried with them a glimmer of hope and a promise of transformation, bound together by the timeless wisdom of the monk's words.

To achieve autonomy, one must strive to become a universe unto oneself, detached from the influences of changing phenomena. An interesting comparison can be drawn to Metatron's cube, a symbol mentioned in ancient Christian, Islamic, and Jewish texts. Metatron is often associated with the Egyptian deity Thoth and the Greek figure Hermes Trismegistus and is closely linked to the Tetragrammaton, which represents the fundamental geometric pattern believed to be the template of physical reality - also referred to as the Word of God or the Logos.

In contemplating Metatron's cube, one can observe a 2-dimensional representation of the figure that, upon a shift in perspective, reveals a 3D cube without any alteration to the figure itself. This transformation in perception highlights how introducing a new dimension can alter one's understanding of a concept. By transcending limited perspectives and embracing a broader viewpoint, true liberation is achieved. This liberation allows individuals to cultivate fresh perspectives without becoming entrenched in or attached to any singular viewpoint.

Throughout history, great minds have emphasized the importance of moving beyond the confines of the self. Albert Einstein, for instance, suggested that the true measure of an individual lies in their ability to attain liberation from the self. It is not the act of thinking or the existence of the self that should be condemned; rather, it is the enslavement to the ego's constant filtering of reality through judgment, preference, and attachment that leads to suffering. The ego-driven mind perpetuates a cycle of craving and aversion, trapping individuals within a web of incessant thoughts and desires.

To break free from this cycle, one must refrain from categorizing thoughts as either good or bad and instead seek to explore their essence beyond the limitations of language and labels. By stripping away all preconceptions and shedding the ego's influence, one can begin to perceive reality as it truly is, unclouded by personal interpretations. Just as a child, once taught what a bird is, may forevermore see only their thoughts rather than the creature itself, so too do many individuals become blinded by their assumptions and beliefs about their wakefulness and consciousness. If one presumes oneself to be awake, why would one undertake the challenging journey to achieve what one mistakenly believes one already possesses?

The path to true awakening requires an unmasking of the self-deception that shrouds our perception. Just as the ancient mystics sought to pierce through the veil of illusion to touch the divine essence within, so too must modern seekers navigate the labyrinth of their minds to uncover the truth that lies beyond the mirage of egoic identification.

In the stillness of introspection, where the echoes of societal conditioning fade into silence, there exists a pristine clarity that illuminates the path to self-realization. It is in this sacred space that one may catch a glimpse of their authentic self, unburdened by the weight of expectations and insecurities that cloak their inner light.

Embracing the essence of Metatron's cube, we can perceive ourselves as multidimensional beings, capable of transcending the limitations of our physical form and mental constructs. The layers of conditioning and programming that once confined our consciousness begin to dissolve, revealing the boundless potential that resides within each of us.

As we journey deeper into the recesses of our being, we begin to unravel the tangled web of beliefs and identities that have defined us for so long. With each thread we release, we inch closer to the core of our existence, where the pure essence of our being shines with a luminosity that transcends all worldly concerns.

It is in this sacred space of self-discovery that we come to understand the true meaning of autonomy - the freedom to express our authentic selves without fear or hesitation. Like Metatron, who bridges the realms of heaven and earth, we, too, find ourselves straddling the threshold between the mundane and the transcendent, embodying the divine blueprint of our true nature.

And so, the journey towards autonomy is not merely a quest for personal empowerment but a sacred odyssey of self-realization that leads us back to the source of all creation. In the light of this awareness, we are no longer mere mortals bound by the confines of time and space, but eternal beings of infinite potential, united in our quest for liberation and enlightenment.

Before one can truly awaken, there must be a recognition that we are existing in a state of slumber, living within the confines of the Matrix. The first step towards awakening involves introspection and an honest evaluation of our lives without deceiving ourselves. Are we able to break free from the monotonous and robotic patterns that dictate our actions? Can we resist the allure of seeking momentary pleasures and evading discomfort? Have we become enslaved by certain foods or habits? Do we find ourselves constantly passing judgment, assigning blame, and criticizing ourselves and others? Is our mind always craving stimulation, or can we find contentment in pure silence? Are we overly concerned with the perceptions of others, craving approval and validation? Do we unknowingly undermine our progress in life?

For many individuals, life unfolds in a repetitive cycle, mirroring the present in the future, a year hence, even a decade down the line. The realization of our mechanical and unconscious existence brings a glimmer of awakening, allowing us to comprehend the gravity of the situation - we are deep in slumber, ensnared in a dreamlike state. Similar to the prisoners in Plato's allegorical cave, most will balk at the prospect of altering their lives, reluctant to release the familiar chains that bind them. We often weave intricate justifications for our behaviors, opting to evade reality rather than face it head-on. We yearn for salvation, yet shy away from bearing the burdens ourselves. What sacrifices are we prepared to make in pursuit of freedom?

To embark on the journey of awakening, we must acknowledge our entanglement with the constructs of the human mind, the facade we wear as our identity of self. A certain part of our essence must resonate with this truth, stirring from its dormant state. Deep within us lies a timeless entity that holds the key to understanding our true nature. The intricate web of the mind captivates us, ensnaring us in a cycle of endless activity, consumption, and desire. This perpetual loop of craving and aversion inhibits the blossoming of our consciousness and obstructs our innate potential for evolutionary growth toward samadhi.

In our contemporary society, pathological thought patterns have been normalized, masquerading as the essence of existence. The core of our being, our divine essence, has been overshadowed by the limited constructs of the self. The profound wisdom and truth of our existence lie buried within us, waiting to be unveiled. As Jiddu Krishnamurti aptly stated, true health is not measured by conformity to a profoundly sick society. The identification with the egoic mind is the ailment, while samadhi serves as the remedy for our collective slumber.

In the depths of contemplation, we find a path to liberation from the shackles of societal conditioning. It is an inward journey, where the ego begins to lose its grip and the veil of illusion lifts. Like a gentle breeze that whispers truths long forgotten, samadhi beckons us to remember our essence beyond the confines of the mind.

In embracing the practice of mindfulness and self-inquiry, we confront the roots of our suffering and transcend them. The cacophony of external expectations fades into the background, giving way to the symphony of our inner wisdom. Through the lens of awareness, we begin to see the interconnectedness of all beings and the vastness of our shared humanity.

True health, as Krishnamurti reminds us, is not found in conformity but in the courageous act of authenticity. It is a journey of self-discovery and self-realization, guided by the light of samadhi. As we navigate the complexities of existence, may we remember that our true nature is love, compassion, and boundless potential.

As we delve deeper into the realms of mindfulness and self-inquiry, we embark on a profound journey of self-discovery and transformation. It is a journey that requires courage and vulnerability as we confront the roots of our suffering with unwavering honesty and compassion. With each mindful breath and introspective questioning, we peel back the layers of conditioned patterns and limiting beliefs that have held us captive for so long.

In the stillness of each moment, the external noise and distractions that once consumed our attention begin to dissipate, allowing the radiant light of our inner wisdom to shine forth. This inner wisdom is not separate from us; it is woven into the fabric of our being, waiting patiently to be uncovered and embraced. Through the practice of mindfulness, we learn to listen deeply to the whispers of our soul, guiding us towards a path of healing and growth.

As we cultivate mindfulness, we also begin to recognize the interconnectedness of all beings and the vast tapestry of our shared humanity. We realize that we are not isolated islands, but interconnected threads in the intricate web of life. Our joy and suffering are intertwined with the joy and suffering of others, reminding us of the inherent oneness that binds us all together.

With this awareness, we are called to extend compassion and kindness not only to ourselves but to all living beings. We understand that our thoughts, words, and actions have a ripple effect that reverberates far beyond our individual lives. By embodying mindfulness and self-inquiry, we become beacons of light and love, illuminating the path for others to follow.

Through the practice of mindfulness and self-inquiry, we learn to embrace the full spectrum of our human experience with grace and acceptance. We no longer resist the ebbs and flows of life but instead flow with the currents, trusting in the inherent wisdom of the universe. In this surrender, we find freedom and liberation from the shackles of our own making.

As we continue to deepen our practice, we uncover hidden truths and insights that were previously obscured by the veil of illusion. We confront our fears and insecurities with courage and compassion, knowing that true healing comes from shining the light of awareness on our shadows. In this process of unraveling, we discover the beauty and resilience that lie at the core of our being, waiting to be embraced and celebrated.

Mindfulness and self-inquiry are not merely practices; they are gateways to our true nature and essence. Through these transformative practices, we awaken to the infinite potential that resides within us, empowering us to live with intention and purpose. We recognize that our journey is a sacred pilgrimage, guided by the inner compass of our hearts.

In the sanctuary of mindfulness and self-inquiry, we find solace and retreat from the hustle and bustle of the outside world. It is here, in the depths of our being, that we discover the peace and serenity that has always been within us. We realize that true fulfillment comes from within, not from external validations or achievements.

As we integrate mindfulness and self-inquiry into our daily lives, we become more attuned to the present moment and the beauty that surrounds us. We savor each breath, each step, and each interaction as a precious gift to be cherished. Our hearts overflow with gratitude and appreciation for the simple miracles that unfold in every moment.

The practice of mindfulness and self-inquiry invites us to lean into discomfort and uncertainty with an open heart and mind. We learn to embrace the transient nature of life, trusting in the inherent wisdom of impermanence. In the face of challenges and obstacles, we stand anchored in our inner strength and resilience, knowing that we have the capacity to weather any storm.

With each mindful pause and reflective inquiry, we deepen our connection to ourselves and the world around us. We discover that the answers we seek are not external but lie within the depths of our own being. By tapping into this wellspring of inner wisdom, we navigate the complexities of life with clarity and discernment.

In the crucible of mindfulness and self-inquiry, we undergo a process of alchemical transformation, transmuting our pain into healing, our fear into courage, and our confusion into clarity. We emerge from this sacred crucible reborn, with a renewed sense of purpose and direction. Our hearts are filled with a profound sense of love and compassion for all beings, knowing that we are interconnected in the vast web of existence.

As we journey further along the path of mindfulness and self-inquiry, we come to embody the qualities of presence, compassion, and equanimity. We meet each moment with an open heart and a curious mind, embracing whatever arises with grace and acceptance. In this state of radical acceptance, we find liberation from the chains of our conditioning and the limitations of our ego.

Mindfulness and self-inquiry become our guiding lights, illuminating the path of awakening and self-realization. We walk this path with humility and gratitude, knowing that we are but humble seekers on the journey of life. With each step, we inch closer to the truth of our being, shedding the layers of illusion and delusion that have clouded our vision for so long.

In the vast expanse of our shared humanity, we find solace in the interconnectedness of all beings. We recognize that we are not separate entities but reflections of the same divine essence. Our hearts beat to the rhythm of the universal heartbeat, pulsating with the energy of love and compassion.

Through the practice of mindfulness and self-inquiry, we cultivate a deep sense of empathy and understanding for the struggles and joys of others. We extend a hand of compassion to those in need, knowing that our liberation is intricately tied to the liberation of all beings. In this interplay of give and take, we experience the transformative power of love and unity.

As we immerse ourselves in the practice of mindfulness and self-inquiry, we become vessels of healing and transformation in the world. We radiate the light of awareness and compassion, uplifting those around us and creating a ripple effect of positivity and inspiration. Our presence becomes a source of solace and guidance for those who are lost in the maze of life.

In the sanctuary of our inner being, we discover the source of true peace and joy that transcends all external circumstances. We realize that happiness is not contingent on external validation or material possessions but springs forth from the well of our own being. With each mindful breath, we inhale the fragrance of inner peace and exhale the burdens of the past.

Mindfulness and self-inquiry are not destinations but ongoing practices that invite us to delve deeper into the mystery of our own being. With each moment of mindfulness, we peel back the layers of illusion and delusion, revealing the shining essence of our true nature. In this journey of self-discovery, we uncover the hidden jewels of wisdom and insight that have been waiting patiently to be unveiled.

As we embrace the practice of mindfulness and self-inquiry, we come to understand that our suffering is not a curse but a gift in disguise. It is through our wounds that the light of awareness enters, illuminating the dark corners of our psyche and revealing the hidden treasures within. With each act of self-inquiry, we dig deeper into the soil of our being, unearthing the roots of our suffering and transforming them into fertile ground for growth.

In the relentless dance of life, we learn to surrender to the flow of existence, trusting in the divine orchestration of the universe. We release our grip on control and surrender to the currents of grace and abundance that carry us forward. With each mindful step, we walk the path of surrender and trust, knowing that we are guided and supported by the vast intelligence of the cosmos.

Mindfulness and self-inquiry are not mere concepts but lived experiences that transform the very fabric of our being. Through the practice of mindfulness, we awaken to the beauty and simplicity of each moment, savoring the richness of life in all its hues. Through self-inquiry, we dive deep into the ocean of our subconscious, unraveling the tangled knots of past traumas and limiting beliefs.

As we integrate mindfulness and self-inquiry into our daily lives, we become architects of our destiny, shaping our reality with intention and clarity. We no longer react to life but respond with wisdom and discernment, anchored in the present moment. We reclaim our power and sovereignty as conscious beings, walking the path of true liberation and freedom.

In the embrace of mindfulness and self-inquiry, we unveil the sacred tapestry of our interconnectedness with all beings. We recognize that we are but reflections of each other, mirroring the same essence of divinity and love. With each act of kindness and compassion, we contribute to the weaving of a new world, one rooted in unity and harmony.

As we journey deeper into the realms of mindfulness and self-inquiry, we shed the layers of conditioning and societal expectations that have masked our true essence. We stand naked and vulnerable, yet liberated and empowered, embracing the fullness of our being with open arms. In this act of radical self-acceptance, we find freedom and peace beyond measure.

Mindfulness and self-inquiry beckon us to dive into the depths of our being to explore the uncharted territories of our psyche with courage and curiosity. In this sacred exploration, we unearth the buried treasures of our soul, discovering the hidden gems of wisdom and insight that the veils of ignorance have obscured. With each mindful breath, we inhale the essence of our being and exhale the illusions that bind us.

In the crucible of mindfulness and self-inquiry, we confront our shadows and fears with courage and compassion, knowing that true healing comes from shining the light of awareness on our darkest corners. We embrace our imperfections and vulnerabilities as sacred gifts, guiding us toward greater authenticity and wholeness. Through this process of radical self-acceptance, we reclaim our power and sovereignty as divine beings, liberated from the chains of self-judgment and criticism.

As we deepen our practice of mindfulness and self-inquiry, we come to embody the qualities of presence, compassion, and equanimity in all our interactions. We listen deeply to the cries of the heart, extending a hand of empathy and understanding to those in need. We hold space for the joys and sorrows of life, embracing them with grace and acceptance. In this way, we become anchors of light and love in a world shrouded in darkness and fear.

Through the practice of mindfulness and self-inquiry, we awaken to the interconnectedness of all beings and the vastness of our shared humanity. We realize that our journeys are but threads in the tapestry of existence, woven together in a beautiful dance of unity and diversity. With each mindful breath, we honor the interplay of light and shadow, knowing that both are essential for the tapestry of life to shine truly.

As we walk the path of mindfulness and self-inquiry, we learn to embrace the present moment with gratitude and appreciation for the gift of life. We savor the simple joys that abound in each moment, recognizing the preciousness of each breath and each heartbeat. Our hearts overflow with love and compassion for all beings, knowing that we are intricately connected in the symphony of existence.

In the sanctuary of mindfulness and self-inquiry, we find refuge and solace from the storms of life, immersing ourselves in the boundless ocean of our own being. It is here, in the stillness of our inner sanctum, that we discover the peace and tranquility that transcend all external circumstances. With each mindful breath, we anchor ourselves in the eternal now, free from the burdens of the past and the worries of the future.

Mindfulness and self-inquiry are not distant ideals but lived experiences that enrich and enliven every aspect of our being. Through the practice of mindfulness, we awaken to the beauty and wonder of the world around us, marveling at the intricate dance of creation unfolding in every moment. Through self-inquiry, we delve deep into the recesses of our soul, unraveling the mysteries that lie hidden beneath the surface.

As we integrate mindfulness and self-inquiry into our daily lives, we become vessels of light and love, radiating the essence of our true nature to all beings. We embody the qualities of compassion and understanding, offering a beacon of hope and inspiration to those in need. With each act of kindness and generosity, we plant seeds of transformation and healing in the fertile soil of our collective consciousness.

In the crucible of mindfulness and self-inquiry, we confront our fears and insecurities with courage and grace, knowing that true freedom comes from facing our inner demons with compassion and acceptance. We embrace the shadows that lurk in the recesses of our psyche, knowing that they hold the keys to our liberation and wholeness. Through this act of radical self-acceptance, we unlock the door to our true essence, unleashing the boundless potential that lies within.

As we journey deeper into the realms of mindfulness and self-inquiry, we come to understand that our suffering is not a curse but a gateway to our awakening. It is through our wounds that the light of awareness enters, illuminating the dark corners of our being and revealing the hidden jewels of wisdom and insight that have been waiting patiently to be unearthed. With each act of self-inquiry, we excavate the buried treasures of our soul, setting them aglow with the radiance of our inner light.

Through the practice of mindfulness and self-inquiry, we learn to dance with the rhythms of life, embracing the full spectrum of our human experience with grace and equanimity. We no longer resist the tides of change but flow with them, trusting in the inherent wisdom of the universe to guide us on our journey. In this surrender, we find true liberation and freedom from the shackles of our own making.

Mindfulness and self-inquiry are not passive endeavors but dynamic processes that invite us to engage with life fully and authentically. With each mindful breath, we infuse our awareness into the present moment, savoring the richness of life in all its flavors. Through self-inquiry, we dive deep into the ocean of our subconscious, plumbing the depths of our psyche for hidden truths and insights.

As we navigate the terrain of mindfulness and self-inquiry, we come to embody the qualities of presence, compassion, and wisdom in all our interactions. We listen deeply to the whispers of the heart, responding with empathy and understanding to the joys and sorrows of those around us. We hold space for the vulnerabilities and fears of others, offering a sanctuary of love and acceptance in a world plagued by judgment and division.

Through the practice of mindfulness and self-inquiry, we cultivate a deep sense of interconnectedness with all beings, recognizing the sacredness of life in its myriad forms. We understand that our journeys are but reflections of the universal journey of awakening and transformation. With each mindful breath, we honor the unity and diversity that make up the tapestry of existence, celebrating the vibrant hues of life in all their beauty.

In the sanctuary of our inner being, we discover the wellspring of peace and joy that flows eternal, independent of external circumstances. We realize that true happiness is not dependent on fleeting pleasures or external validations but springs forth from the essence of our being. With each mindful breath, we tap into the reservoir of inner peace and serenity that resides within us, anchoring ourselves in the eternal now.

Mindfulness and self-inquiry are not destination points but gateways to our true nature and essence. Through the practice of mindfulness, we awaken to the boundless potential that lies within us, empowering us to live with intention and purpose. Through self-inquiry, we excavate the buried treasures of our soul, uncovering the hidden gems of wisdom and insight that the veil of ignorance has obscured.

As we walk the path of mindfulness and self-inquiry, we come to understand that our suffering is not a burden but a gift in disguise. It is through our wounds that the light of awareness enters, illuminating the dark corners of our psyche and revealing the hidden gems of wisdom and insight that have been waiting patiently to be unearthed. With each act of self-inquiry, we excavate the buried treasures of our soul, setting them aglow with the brilliance of our inner light.

Through the practice of mindfulness and self-inquiry, we learn to embrace the full spectrum of our human experience with grace and equanimity. We no longer fear the shadows or shy away from the darkness but instead welcome them as sacred messengers guiding us toward greater wholeness and integration. In this dance of light and shadow, we find balance and harmony, knowing that both are essential for our growth and evolution.

With each mindful breath and introspective inquiry, we deepen our connection to ourselves and the world around us. We uncover hidden truths and insights that were previously obscured by the veil of illusion, shedding light on the path of self-discovery and transformation. In the crucible of mindfulness and self-inquiry, we undergo a process of alchemical transformation, transmuting our pain into healing, our fear into courage, and our confusion into clarity.

As we integrate mindfulness and self-inquiry into our daily lives, we become vessels of light and love, radiating the essence of our true nature to all beings. We embody the qualities of presence, compassion, and equanimity, offering a beacon of hope and inspiration to those in need. We walk the path of awakening and liberation with grace and humility, knowing that we are but humble travelers on the journey of life.

In the vast expanse of our shared humanity, we find solace in the interconnectedness of all beings and the oneness that binds us together. We recognize that we are not separate entities but reflections of the same divine essence, pulsating with the energy of love and compassion. With each mindful breath, we honor the interplay of light and shadow, knowing that both are essential for the transformation and evolution of our collective consciousness.

Mindfulness and self-inquiry are not mere practices but sacred rituals that invite us to dive deep into the mystery of our own being. Through the practice of mindfulness, we awaken to the beauty and wonder of existence, marveling at the intricate dance of creation unfolding in every moment. Through self-inquiry, we excavate the buried treasures of our soul, uncovering the wisdom and insight that lie hidden beneath the surface.

As we embrace the practice of mindfulness and self-inquiry, we come to understand that our suffering is not a curse but a catalyst for growth and transformation. It is through our wounds that the light of awareness enters, illuminating the dark corners of our psyche and revealing the hidden jewels of wisdom and insight that have been waiting patiently to be unveiled. With each act of self-inquiry, we excavate the buried treasures of our soul, setting them aglow with the radiance of our inner light.

Through the practice of mindfulness and self-inquiry, we learn to dance with the rhythms of life, surrendering to the tides of change and transformation with grace and equanimity. We no longer resist the currents of existence but flow with them, trusting in the divine orchestration of the universe to guide us on our path. In this surrender, we find freedom and liberation from the shackles of our own making, stepping into the fullness of our being with courage and conviction.

Mindfulness and self-inquiry are not abstract concepts but lived experiences that enrich and enliven every facet of our existence. Through the practice of mindfulness, we awaken to the beauty and wonder of the world around us, marveling at the intricate interplay of light and shadow in the tapestry of life. Through self-inquiry, we dive deep into the ocean of our subconscious, uncovering the hidden truths and insights that lie beneath the surface.

As we integrate mindfulness and self-inquiry into our daily lives, we become architects of our reality, shaping our destiny with intention and clarity. We no longer react to the challenges of life but respond with wisdom and discernment, anchored in the present moment. We reclaim our power and sovereignty as conscious beings, walking the path of

True health, as Krishnamurti reminds us, is not found in conformity but in the courageous act of authenticity. It is a journey of self-discovery and self-realization, guided by the light of samadhi. As we navigate the complexities of existence, may we remember that our true nature is love, compassion, and boundless potential.

A Meditation on Sumadhi

As the sun slowly set over the horizon, casting a warm golden glow across the tranquil landscape, a sense of peace descended upon the small village nestled in the valley. The gentle rustling of leaves in the breeze seemed to whisper ancient wisdom, reminding the villagers of the timeless truths that lay embedded in the fabric of existence.

In this serene setting, an old sage named Krishnamurti sat under the shade of a towering banyan tree, his gaze serene and all-encompassing, as if he could see beyond the veil of reality into the depths of eternity. His presence exuded a sense of inner calm and profound wisdom, drawing seekers from far and wide who yearned to tap into the wellspring of enlightenment that seemed to flow through him effortlessly.

One such seeker, a young man named Arjun, had traveled for days through rugged terrain and dense forests to reach the village and seek the guidance of the venerable sage. He carried with him the weight of uncertainty and the burden of unanswered questions that had haunted his restless mind for years. As he approached Krishnamurti, a sense of reverence and awe washed over him, mingled with a glimmer of hope that perhaps, in the presence of this wise sage, he would find the answers he sought.

Krishnamurti looked at Arjun with eyes that seemed to penetrate the depths of his soul, as if reading the hidden stories written in the lines of his face and the shadows of his eyes. With a gentle smile, he motioned for Arjun to sit beside him under the spreading branches of the banyan tree, where the air was thick with the perfume of blossoms and the soft hum of insects.

"Welcome, young seeker," Krishnamurti's voice was like a gentle breeze that carried the whispers of eternity. "What troubles your heart, and what brings you to me on this auspicious day?"

Arjun felt a surge of emotion rising within him, a mixture of trepidation and longing, as he began to pour out his innermost thoughts and fears to the sage. He spoke of his struggles with self-doubt and insecurity, of the pain of unfulfilled desires and the relentless pursuit of material success that had left him feeling empty and lost. He bared his soul to Krishnamurti, seeking solace and guidance in the depths of his wisdom.

Krishnamurti listened with a deep sense of compassion and understanding, his eyes reflecting the flickering flame of a hidden truth that shimmered just beyond the veil of illusion. When Arjun fell silent, his voice choked with emotion, the sage spoke again, his words carrying the weight of centuries of wisdom.

"True health, as I remind you, is not found in conformity but in the courageous act of authenticity," Krishnamurti's voice resonated with a power that seemed to echo through the very fabric of existence. "It is a journey of self-discovery and self-realization, guided by the light of samadhi. As we navigate the complexities of existence, may we remember that our true nature is love, compassion, and boundless potential."

Arjun felt a spark of recognition kindling in the depths of his being, a flicker of understanding that seemed to illuminate the shadows of his confusion. In the presence of Krishnamurti, he felt the veils of illusion melting away, revealing glimpses of a deeper reality that had always been present, waiting to be acknowledged.

Days turned into weeks, and Arjun remained by Krishnamurti's side, soaking in the wisdom that flowed from the sage like a river of light. He learned to quiet his restless mind and listen to the whispers of his own heart, to trust in the innate wisdom that resided within him, waiting to be awakened.

Under the guidance of Krishnamurti, Arjun began to peel away the layers of conditioning and false beliefs that had clouded his vision for so long. He delved deep into the recesses of his soul, confronting his fears and insecurities with courage and compassion, embracing the shadows that lurked in the corners of his being.

Through the practices of meditation and self-inquiry, Arjun began to experience moments of profound clarity and insight, where the boundaries of the self dissolved into the vast expanse of eternity. He felt a deep sense of connection with all of creation, an oneness that transcended the limitations of time and space.

As he journeyed deeper into the realms of self-discovery, Arjun encountered the hidden treasures that lay buried within his own being – the seeds of creativity, the wellsprings of compassion, and the infinite potential that awaited his touch. He realized that true health was not merely the absence of disease but a state of wholeness that encompassed body, mind, and spirit in perfect harmony.

Under the guidance of Krishnamurti, Arjun learned to cultivate a sense of gratitude for the blessings that surrounded him – the beauty of nature, the love of family and friends, and the gift of life itself. He understood that true abundance was not measured in material possessions but in the richness of the soul and the depth of connection with the world around him.

In the quiet moments of contemplation, as the world shimmered in the golden light of dawn, Arjun felt a profound sense of peace settling within him, like a gentle rain that nourished the parched earth. He realized that true happiness was not to be found in the pursuit of external pleasures but in the inner tranquility that arose from a deep understanding of the self.

Krishnamurti observed Arjun's transformation with a knowing smile, like a gardener watching a tender shoot unfurl its petals in the warmth of the sun. He knew that the seeds of wisdom had taken root in Arjun's heart, blossoming into the radiant flower of enlightenment that would illuminate his path for years to come.

And so, in the timeless dance of existence, Arjun and Krishnamurti walked together along the path of self-discovery, their footsteps echoing in harmony with the rhythms of the universe. They knew that the journey was endless, the destination ever receding on the horizon, but in the eternal present moment, they found the peace that transcended all understanding.

As the days turned into months and the seasons changed, Arjun continued to explore the depths of his being, guided by the light of Krishnamurti's wisdom that shone like a beacon in the darkness. He knew that the road ahead was fraught with challenges and uncertainties, but he walked it with a sense of courage and grace, trusting in the truth that resided at the core of his being.

And in the golden light of twilight, as the shadows lengthened and the stars began to twinkle in the velvet sky, Arjun whispered a silent prayer of gratitude to the sage who had shown him the way – the way of authenticity, the way of love, the way of boundless potential.

And in that sacred moment, as the breeze carried the fragrance of blossoms and the echoes of ancient wisdom, Arjun knew that he had found true health – not in conformity, but in the courageous act of authenticity, guided by the light of samadhi. And in that realization, he found peace.

THE ENTRANCE TO THE PATH

As we delve deeper into the realms of introspection, we uncover the hidden treasures of our soul waiting to be discovered. It is in these moments of profound contemplation that we realize the limitations imposed upon us by the external world are merely illusions, clouding our perception of the true self that lies within. With each passing breath, we inch closer to a state of samadhi, where the boundaries between the ego and the higher self blur into a harmonious dance of unity. The journey inward is not an easy one, for it demands a surrender of the familiar constructs that have defined our existence for so long. It requires a willingness to let go of the masks we wear, the roles we play, and the expectations we carry like burdens on our shoulders. In this sacred space of self-discovery, we confront our deepest fears and insecurities, peeling away the layers of conditioning to reveal the raw essence of our being. As the ego begins to lose its grip, we are confronted with the stark realization that much of what we have believed to be true about ourselves and the world around us is nothing more than a facade. Like a crumbling wall, the illusions we have built to protect our fragile egos come crashing down, leaving us exposed and vulnerable. And yet, in this vulnerability lies our greatest strength – the courage to face our inner demons and embrace the light that shines within us.

Samadhi, with its ethereal presence, calls out to us like a distant melody, urging us to remember who we truly are beyond the confines of the mind. It is a state of blissful awareness where the boundaries of time and space dissolve, and we become one with the infinite cosmic energy that flows through all of creation. In this transcendent state, we realize that we are not separate from the universe but interconnected threads in the grand tapestry of existence. Through the practice of meditation and mindfulness, we learn to quiet the incessant chatter of the mind and sink into the stillness that resides at the core of our being. It is in these moments of silence that the whispers of truth become clear, guiding us toward a deeper understanding of ourselves and the world around us. As we gaze upon the reflection of our soul in the mirror of consciousness, we are filled with a sense of wonder and awe at the divine beauty that resides within us. The journey to samadhi is a transformative one, for it requires us to confront our shadows and embrace our light with equal measure. It is a process of integration and reconciliation, where we come to terms with the dualities that exist within us and find balance in the midst of chaos.

Through the alchemy of self-discovery, we transmute our pain into wisdom, our fears into courage, and our doubts into faith. As we traverse the inner landscape of our soul, we encounter the archetypes and symbols that populate the collective unconscious, reflecting back to us the universal truths that bind us all together. We see ourselves mirrored in the myths and legends of ancient civilizations, recognizing the timeless wisdom that has been passed down through the ages. In these stories of gods and goddesses, heroes and villains, we find echoes of our struggles and triumphs, pointing the way toward our heroic journey of self-realization. The path to liberation is not a sprint but a marathon, requiring patience, perseverance, and unwavering dedication to the pursuit of spiritual growth. It is a lifelong journey of self-discovery and self-mastery, where each step taken brings us closer to the realization of our true potential. As we navigate the twists and turns of the spiritual path, we encounter challenges and obstacles that test our resolve and fortitude, pushing us to confront our limitations and fears head-on. In the crucible of transformation, we are reborn anew, shedding the old skin of our former selves and stepping into the radiant light of our higher consciousness. Like a phoenix rising from the ashes, we emerge stronger and more resilient, with a renewed sense of purpose and clarity of vision. In this state of awakened awareness, we see the world with fresh eyes, free from the distortions of the past and open to the infinite possibilities that lie before us.

As we continue on our journey toward samadhi, we cultivate a sense of inner peace and serenity that transcends the external circumstances of our lives. We learn to navigate the ebbs and flows of existence with grace and equanimity, knowing that all experiences – whether pleasant or challenging – are but fleeting moments in the grand tapestry of our soul's evolution. With each breath, we draw closer to the divine essence that resides within us, aligning our individual will with the greater cosmic purpose that guides us along our path. In the stillness of samadhi, we find solace and refuge from the stormy seas of life, anchoring ourselves in the eternal presence of the here and now. It is in this sacred space of inner silence that we commune with the divine source of all creation, feeling the pulsating heartbeat of the universe reverberate within our hearts. In this union of self and divinity, we experience a state of blissful union that transcends words and concepts, a state of pure being that defies rational explanation. As we bask in the radiance of samadhi, we are filled with a profound sense of gratitude and humility, knowing that we are but channels through which the light of the divine flows into the world. We surrender our personal will to the greater cosmic will, becoming instruments of universal love and compassion in a world desperate for healing and transformation. With each act of kindness and generosity, we sow seeds of peace and harmony that ripple outwards, touching the hearts of all beings and igniting the flames of awakening within them. In the boundless expanse of samadhi, we find liberation from the confines of the ego and the illusions of separateness that have plagued humanity for millennia. We realize that we are not isolated individuals but interconnected threads in the vast web of life, each one essential to the greater whole. In this realization of our oneness with all of creation, we embrace the sacredness of every moment, honoring the divine spark that shines within us and within each living being we encounter.

As we journey deeper into the mysteries of samadhi, we come to understand that the ultimate truth is not something to be grasped with the intellect but experienced with the heart. It is a knowing that transcends words and concepts, a gnosis that arises from the depths of our being and permeates every fiber of our existence. In this state of awakened awareness, we are no longer bound by the limitations of the mind but soar on the wings of divine consciousness, merging with the eternal source of all life. In the final moments of samadhi, as we stand on the threshold of liberation, we are enveloped in a radiant light that bathes us in its effulgent glow. We feel ourselves dissolve into the cosmic ocean of consciousness, becoming one with the infinite expanse of being that stretches out before us. In this moment of divine union, we realize that we are not separate from the divine but are, in fact, an integral part of its eternal essence, forever united in the dance of creation and destruction. And so, we return from the depths of contemplation, our souls ablaze with the fire of divine love and wisdom. We step back into the world, renewed and transformed, ready to share the gifts of our inner journey with all those we meet along the way. With each word spoken, each action taken, we serve as beacons of light in a world shrouded in darkness, guiding others toward the path of liberation and enlightenment. And in this sacred dance of life, we find our true purpose – to awaken to the infinite potential that lies within us and to help others do the same.

DEVINE GAME OF LILA

A self-discovery tool

In ancient Hindu teachings, this principle is known as the "Devine Game of Lila." Lila, which translates to "Game" from Sanskrit, encourages viewing life as a playful experience and approaching each moment with an open heart. The Game of Leela is a self-discovery tool that allows you to "test the route" and, if necessary, adjust your direction of movement. Through Lila, we delve deeper into our wisdom and find answers to life's myriad questions. The concept of Lila suggests that an objective does not drive creation but rather emerges from the divine's playful essence. This underscores a sense of freedom rather than necessity in the act of creation.

The notion of Lila resonates across various schools of Indian philosophy, both non-dualist and dualist. In non-dualism, Lila embodies the idea that all existence, including the cosmos, arises from the creative play of the divine absolute, Brahman. Within Vaishnavism, Lila encompasses the actions of God and devotees, as well as the grand cosmic events in the manifest universe.

Human consciousness exists on a continuum, ranging from complete identification with the material self to the ultimate awakening and the dissolution of the self. Progressing towards awakening on this continuum leads to a reduction in self-induced suffering. It's important to note that experiencing less suffering does not equate to a life devoid of pain. Awakening transcends the dualities of pain and pleasure, resulting in a diminished presence of the mind, cravings, attachments, and resistance to unfolding events.

The cessation of the self-structure during awakening reveals a state devoid of egoic thoughts, self-identity, or duality. However, a sense of "I am," anatta, or non-self persists in this awakened state. This emptiness signals the emergence of Prajna, the highest form of wisdom, knowledge, and understanding. Prajna surpasses mere intellectual reasoning and inference, emphasizing a profound insight into the immanent self beyond duality and the entire continuum.

In this realm of Prajna, one's consciousness expands beyond the limitations of the physical world, transcending the boundaries of ordinary perception. It is here, amidst the infinite vastness of wisdom, that clarity dawns like a radiant sun upon the horizon of the mind. Every question finds its answer, every doubt dissolves into certainty.

The very fabric of existence is woven with threads of Prajna, guiding the seeker towards a deeper realization of the interconnectedness of all things. No longer bound by the constraints of time and space, the seeker wanders through the labyrinthine corridors of universal truth with a sense of awe and reverence.

Within the silence of Prajna's domain, the heartbeat of the cosmos pulsates in harmony with the rhythm of the seeker's own soul. Each breath is a mantra, each step a sacred pilgrimage towards the sanctum of eternal wisdom. And in this sacred communion, the seeker discovers the profound beauty of simply being, of existing in perfect alignment with the cosmic dance of creation.

This understanding extends to the perception of emptiness within each phenomenon, highlighting the absence of inherent selfhood according to Buddhist teachings. Buddhism challenges the concept of a permanent, unchanging self and asserts that all phenomena lack intrinsic identities. The Buddhist perspective emphasizes interdependence and impermanence, viewing emptiness as the ultimate reality of the world. Through the doctrines of emptiness, Buddhism elucidates the transient nature of the self and the senselessness of all existence.

Once upon a time in the ancient land of Pataliputra, the renowned Buddhist philosopher Nāgārjuna delved deep into the esoteric teachings of the sutras. His wisdom was revered far and wide, and seekers of truth flocked to hear his enlightening words. One day, a young monk approached Nāgārjuna with a burning question that had been troubling his mind. "Venerable Nāgārjuna," the monk began, "how can one attain true liberation from the cycle of samsara?" Nāgārjuna smiled gently, his eyes filled with profound compassion. "Dear child," he began, "the path to liberation is a journey of self-realization and understanding. One must cultivate wisdom, compassion, and mindfulness in all actions." The monk listened intently as Nāgārjuna spoke of the Middle Way and the interconnected nature of all things. His words were like a soothing balm to the monk's restless soul, guiding him on the path towards enlightenment. From that day on, the young monk dedicated himself to the teachings of Nāgārjuna, striving to embody the principles of non-attachment and impermanence. And as he walked the path laid out by the great philosopher, he found peace, wisdom, and ultimately, liberation from the cycle of suffering. And so, the legacy of Nāgārjuna lived on through the hearts and minds of those who sought the profound truths he shared, inspiring generations to come in their quest for spiritual enlightenment.

The renowned Buddhist philosopher Nāgārjuna, a key figure in the Mādhyamika school, famously proclaimed the elusive nature of intrinsic essence within all phenomena. This assertion emphasizes the absence of inherent substance in the tangible and conceptual facets of our perceived reality. Consequently, the foundation of our understanding shifts into a realm devoid of substantiality. Within each dhárma or phenomenon, the absence of a self is evident, aligning with Buddhist teachings that classify them as śūnya or empty. Buddhism advocates for the sincere pursuit of this truth, asserting that the world lacks essence or self. Jizang, the architect of East Asian Mādhyamika, emphasizes that enlightenment hinges on grasping this absence of essence or self. By recognizing the inherent emptiness in every phenomenon, individuals can attain enlightenment and gain insight into the fabric of reality.

The legacy of the renowned Buddhist philosopher Nāgārjuna echoes through the corridors of time, resonating with profound wisdom and insight. At the heart of the Mādhyamika school lies his bold declaration – the elusive nature of intrinsic essence that permeates all facets of existence. In a world where tangible and conceptual realms intertwine, Nāgārjuna's teachings challenge us to traverse the boundless expanse of reality stripped of its supposed substance.

Within the intricate tapestry of dhármas, the absence of a fixed self lingers, casting shadows upon our conventional understanding. Embracing the doctrine of emptiness, Buddhism sheds light on the impermanent nature of all things. This fundamental truth beckons seekers to navigate a path that leads beyond the illusory veil of selfhood.

Jizang, the visionary behind the East Asian Mādhyamika, emphasizes that enlightenment beckons those who dare to confront the void within each phenomenon. By peering into the abyss of emptiness, individuals unearth the seeds of enlightenment and unravel the mysteries woven into the fabric of existence. In this realm of flux and impermanence, the absence of essence reveals itself as the gateway to profound realization and clarity.

DISCOVERING THE SELF

The first steps to the inner journey

You are always growing and changing based on your personality and life experiences. Therefore, it's important to take time out to conduct a self-analysis periodically. Self-analyses help you to reflect on where you are in various aspects of your life. Armed with this information, you are better prepared to make necessary adjustments as you move forward in life.

When I began my quest, I began identifying my belief structures. I approached the journey from a strictly ideological aspect. I was led by the egoic construct and delved into soaking up as much knowledge on ideologies that I could process. The more I learned the more I craved. My ego fueled this craving. It was not until I began understanding all aspects of Buddhism that I realized that the steps to understanding all there was about who I am had been laid out by one of the greatest teachers ever to walk the earth. However, your adventure does not have to begin in such a profound way.

It can be incredibly difficult to disconnect from our true selves in a world that always requires our focus. The busy and chaotic nature of everyday life may overpower the peaceful inner voice, causing feelings of disconnection and lack of fulfilment. However, undertaking a deep exploration of oneself is one of the most meaningful and satisfying pursuits we can engage in. This voyage entails uncovering our true essence by removing the layers of conditioning, beliefs, and societal expectations.

Self-Analysis Model in Western Psychology

In the realm of psychological science, self-awareness holds a significant place as a cornerstone for personal growth and emotional well-being. It aids in comprehending our behaviors, emotions, and thought processes, facilitating informed decision-making and stronger relationships. Among the most potent methods to enhance self-awareness lies in the realm of reflecting psychology, commonly referred to as self-reflection. In this all-encompassing guide, we aim to navigate the realm of self-reflection, shedding light on its essence, advantages, and diverse techniques to empower you in mastering the skill of self-awareness.

Self-reflection serves as a powerful tool in the journey of self-awareness, guiding individuals toward a deeper understanding of their inner workings. By delving into the realms of one's thoughts, emotions, and behaviors, the path to personal growth becomes clearer, illuminated by the light of introspection.

The advantages of self-reflection are manifold, offering a mirror through which individuals can gain insights into their strengths, weaknesses, and aspirations. This process paves the way for informed decision-making as individuals become more attuned to their values and beliefs, aligning their actions with their authentic selves.

Embarking on the practice of self-reflection opens avenues for self-improvement and heightened emotional intelligence. Through journaling, meditation, or simply taking moments of quiet contemplation, individuals can unravel the complexities of their psyche, fostering resilience and self-compassion in the face of challenges.

As we venture into the depths of self-reflection, we invite you to explore the myriad techniques at your disposal. From mindfulness practices to guided introspective exercises, the journey of self-awareness is as unique as the individual undertaking it. May this guide be your compass, guiding you towards a more profound understanding of yourself and those around you, heralding a newfound sense of clarity and purpose in the tapestry of your life.

What is Self-Reflection?

Embarking on the inner journey involves exploring one's innermost thoughts, feelings, convictions, and past experiences to gain a deeper understanding of the true self. Unlike pursuits of material gain or social status, the inner journey emphasizes self-reflection and the pursuit of inner peace and fulfillment. This journey is highly personalized, reflecting individual experiences, cultural influences, and aspirations while also encompassing universal themes and techniques to guide individuals in their introspective endeavors.

Embarking on a journey into the depths of psychological reflection requires a foundational understanding of self-reflection. In essence, self-reflection involves delving into one's thoughts, emotions, behaviors, and motivations. It necessitates stepping back from the hustle and bustle of everyday life, suspending judgment, and turning inward to gain insight and understanding about oneself.

Self-reflection acts as a mental mirror that enables individuals to perceive their inner selves with heightened clarity. It involves the practice of introspection and deep contemplation about one's own experiences and actions. Through the cultivation of self-reflection, individuals can develop a more profound understanding of their self-concept, emotional states, and cognitive processes.

The central aim of the self-analysis model is to elucidate how individuals construct, uphold, and adjust their "self-concepts." These self-concepts are essentially representations or "identity images" that pertain to various aspects of a person's abilities, behavioral tendencies, beliefs, values, emotional responses, status, and desires. These representations can exist at different levels of abstraction, with most representing specific actions or responses related to particular situations or tasks.

Self-concepts comprise both descriptive and evaluative components. The descriptive aspect pertains to the content of the identity image, such as characteristics like physical attractiveness or ambition. Most self-concepts are individualizing in nature, deviating from the ordinary either in a positive or negative direction. The evaluative facet of self-concept relates to the perceived value or appropriateness of an identity image, considering factors like commandability or societal acceptance.

The evaluation of self-concepts is largely influenced by social norms, which can elevate seemingly trivial traits or devalue crucial characteristics based on societal perceptions. Cultural norms and societal expectations play a pivotal role in shaping the evaluation of self-concepts, determining what is considered valuable or admirable within a given society.

While individuals tend to maintain stable conceptions of their core self-concepts or facets linked to their self-worth, other self-concepts are constructed dynamically in response to situational demands. The formation of self-concepts can be influenced by various factors such as personal experiences, social comparisons, and cultural norms.

The self-analysis model aligns with the framework of social comparison theory, which explores how individuals engage in comparisons with others to evaluate themselves. Social comparison theory encompasses a broad range of topics, including the antecedents and consequences of comparisons, individual differences in comparison tendencies, and the influence of emotions like envy and jealousy on comparison processes.

Comparison tests serve as tools for individuals to assess their characteristics and prospects, involving the estimation of relative positions between oneself and a standard or target. These tests can be intrapersonal, involving comparisons of an individual's attributes over time, or interpersonal, comparing attributes among different individuals. Comparison tests can also involve abstract targets or hypothetical scenarios, contributing to the development of self-concepts.

In addition to selecting and interpreting comparison tests, individuals engage in the essential task of translating the acquired data into enduring self-concepts. This process involves navigating tasks and social feedback to achieve a balance between accurate self-assessment and maintaining positive self-regard. The impact of comparison tests can vary in terms of their influence on related self-concepts, depending on factors like reliability, validity, and individual goals.

Self-analysis may be prompted not only by specific events or outcomes but also by the desire to clarify and refine self-concepts. Individuals may engage in self-analysis as they navigate important life decisions or confront significant challenges, leading to deeper introspection and self-evaluation.

The availability of comparison opportunities and the nature of comparison tests play crucial roles in shaping individuals' self-perceptions and self-concepts. While deliberate comparisons of physical and intellectual abilities are common, social and emotional comparisons often unfold spontaneously in everyday interactions and situations. The direction and range of comparison opportunities can impact how individuals perceive themselves relative to others.

Embarking on the inner journey involves exploring one's innermost thoughts, feelings, convictions, and past experiences to gain a deeper understanding of the true self. Unlike pursuits of material gain or social status, the inner journey emphasizes self-reflection and the pursuit of inner peace and fulfillment. This journey is highly personalized, reflecting individual experiences, cultural influences, and aspirations while also encompassing universal themes and techniques to guide individuals in their introspection.

Self-reflection serves as a powerful tool in the journey of self-awareness, guiding individuals toward a deeper understanding of their inner workings. By delving into the realms of one's thoughts, emotions, and behaviors, the path to personal growth becomes clearer, illuminated by the light of introspection.

The advantages of self-reflection are manifold, offering a mirror through which individuals can gain insights into their strengths, weaknesses, and aspirations. This process paves the way for informed decision-making as individuals become more attuned to their values and beliefs, aligning their actions with their authentic selves.

Embarking on the practice of self-reflection opens avenues for self-improvement and heightened emotional intelligence. Through journaling, meditation, or simply taking moments of quiet contemplation, individuals can unravel the complexities of their psyche, fostering resilience and self-compassion in the face of challenges.

As we venture into the depths of self-reflection, we invite you to explore the myriad techniques at your disposal. From mindfulness practices to guided introspective exercises, the journey of self-awareness is as unique as the individual undertaking it. May this guide be your compass, guiding you towards a more profound understanding of yourself and those around you, heralding a newfound sense of clarity and purpose in the tapestry of your life.

Reflecting Western and Eastern Psychology in Practice

Now that we understand the importance of self-reflection let's explore some practical ways to incorporate reflecting psychology into your daily life:

1. Journaling

Keeping a journal is one of the most effective methods of self-reflection. Write down your thoughts, feelings, and experiences regularly. You can also use journaling prompts to guide your reflection and foster consistency.

2. Reflective Listening

In your interactions with others, practice reflective listening. This involves paraphrasing and summarizing what the other person has said to show that you understand their perspective. This not only helps you improve your listening skills but also encourages self-reflection as you process their words.

3. Setting Aside Judgment

When engaging in self-reflection, it's essential to set aside judgment. Avoid being overly critical of yourself and strive for self-compassion. This allows for a more honest and constructive reflection process.

Step 1.

- The internal journey involves developing self-awareness, which is the ability to observe thoughts, emotions, and behaviors without judgment. This practice allows individuals to understand their motivations, recognize strengths and weaknesses, and identify limiting patterns. Various methods can help in developing self-awareness, such as mindfulness meditation, journaling, and daily self-reflection.

- Mindfulness meditation entails focusing on the present moment without criticism, which can enhance awareness of one's thoughts and emotions. Keeping a journal is an effective way to explore inner thoughts and emotions, enabling individuals to analyze experiences, identify patterns, and gain insights into themselves. Engaging in daily self-reflection by asking questions like, "What did I learn about myself today?" or "How did I experience different emotions in various situations?" can lead to deeper self-understanding. By embracing these practices, individuals can embark on a journey of self-discovery and personal growth.

Step 2: Recognizing fundamental values and convictions.

- Upon embarking on the journey of self-awareness, the next crucial step is to identify and acknowledge your fundamental values and beliefs. These deeply ingrained principles and beliefs are the guiding forces behind the decisions you make and the actions you take. Understanding your values and beliefs is essential as it enables you to align your life in accordance with what truly matters to you.

- Various strategies can help you recognize your fundamental values and beliefs. One such approach involves engaging in exercises that prompt you to pinpoint the values that resonate most with you and then selecting the top five that hold the greatest significance in your life.

- Furthermore, it's imperative to contemplate your beliefs about yourself, others, and the world. Taking the time to delve into the origins of these beliefs and assessing whether they contribute positively to your overall well-being is crucial. It's also important to identify and challenge any limiting beliefs that may be impeding your personal growth.
- Once you have identified your fundamental values, the next step is to live in alignment with them actively. Strive to make decisions and take actions that reflect these values and observe how this alignment impacts your overall satisfaction and health. By living according to your values, you can cultivate a sense of purpose and fulfillment in your life.

Step 3: Accepting Vulnerability.

- Embracing vulnerability is a crucial element of the internal journey, demanding honesty about one's thoughts, emotions, and experiences with oneself and others, even when it feels uncomfortable. This practice is essential for authentic self-exploration and for forming meaningful connections with those around us.

Step 4: To navigate vulnerability effectively, there are several strategies one can adopt.

- Sincere Communication: One should engage in open and honest communication with both themselves and others. By expressing genuine thoughts and emotions, even when they are challenging, individuals can foster deeper and more authentic relationships.
- Self-Compassion: It is important to treat oneself with kindness and understanding, especially during vulnerable moments. Recognizing that vulnerability is a natural part of the human experience and that it takes courage to be open

and honest can help individuals navigate their vulnerabilities with greater ease.

- Seeking Support: Surrounding oneself with compassionate and supportive individuals who can offer a safe space to express vulnerabilities is key. Whether it's friends, family, or a therapist, having a strong support system can aid in accepting and navigating vulnerability effectively.

Step 5: Delving into one's inner desires and passions.

- Exploring the depths of your inner desires and passions is an essential journey toward unveiling your true self. These are the elements that ignite happiness, contentment, and a sense of purpose within you. By embracing and pursuing these passions, you open the door to a more abundant and enriching life experience.
- There are various practices that can aid you in delving into your innermost desires and passions. Engaging in creative endeavors such as writing, painting, dancing, or creating music can serve as a conduit to connect with your innermost desires and passions. By immersing yourself in these artistic expressions, you allow your true essence to shine through.
- Additionally, stepping out of your comfort zone and trying new activities and experiences can lead to the discovery of hidden passions and interests that may have been lying dormant within you. Embrace the uncertainty that comes with exploring the unknown and challenge yourself to break free from familiar constraints.
- Reflecting on moments of pure joy

Step 6: Releasing Yourself from Outside Pressure.

- An essential part of the internal journey involves letting go of external pressures and societal expectations. Many of us have been conditioned to seek validation and approval from others, leading us away from our true selves. By freeing ourselves from these external influences, we can live a more authentic and fulfilling life.

- To release ourselves from external expectations, it is important to practice mindfulness and detachment from the opinions and expectations of others. Focus on what truly matters to you instead of constantly seeking approval from external sources.
- Setting healthy boundaries is crucial in protecting your inner space. Learn to say no to opportunities that do not align with your values and aspirations, prioritizing your own well-being.
- Furthermore, building your self-worth and recognizing your achievements is key. Understand that you are enough just as you are, without needing constant validation from external sources. Embrace your uniqueness and accomplishments, celebrating your individuality.

Step 7: Accepting Change and Expansion.

- Embarking on the inner journey is a journey of constant growth and change. Embracing change and staying open to personal development are essential in unraveling and nurturing your true self.
- To navigate this journey effectively, it is crucial to commit to lifelong learning and self-improvement. Seek opportunities to expand your knowledge and skills and remain open to new perspectives and ideas.
- Developing resilience is another key aspect of this journey. Build coping mechanisms to navigate through adversities and challenges, recognizing that progress often stems from overcoming obstacles.
- It is important to acknowledge and celebrate your achievements, no matter how small they may seem. Each step

taken in your inner exploration is significant and worthy of recognition. By embracing change, fostering growth, and honoring your progress, you can truly embark on a transformative inner journey.

CONCLUSION

Beginning the internal exploration to uncover the true self is a process that brings about profound change and great satisfaction. The process is as individual as fingerprints are to others. Through developing self-awareness, recognizing fundamental values and beliefs, being open to vulnerability, exploring inner desires and passions, releasing external expectations, and embracing change and growth, you can discover your true essence and lead a more genuine and satisfying life. Keep in mind that this experience is specific to you, and there is no correct or incorrect path to take.

Have patience with yourself and let things happen naturally. The process is a marathon and should not be enacted in a way that creates longing and attainment. While delving deeper into your inner self, you will realize that the process is equally valuable compared to the outcome. Welcome the journey and savor the deep revelations that are waiting for you on the road to understanding yourself.

Embarking on the journey of self-discovery is a transformative process that holds the potential to bring about significant changes and a sense of fulfillment. This internal exploration is a deeply personal endeavor akin to uncovering the unique fingerprint of one's essence.

By cultivating self-awareness, acknowledging core values and beliefs, embracing vulnerability, delving into inner passions, letting go of external expectations, and embracing growth and change, individuals can unearth their true selves and live authentically. It is essential to understand that this process is highly individualized, with no fixed guidelines or predetermined outcomes. Patience and a willingness to allow the process to unfold naturally are crucial aspects of this journey. Rather than rushing towards a destination, it is vital to appreciate the value inherent in the process itself. Each step taken towards self-discovery brings with it its revelations and insights, enriching the individual along the way. Self-awareness serves as a foundational element in the quest for self-discovery.

By developing an understanding of one's thoughts, emotions, and behaviors, individuals can gain insight into their inner workings and motivations. This introspective awareness allows individuals to recognize patterns, tendencies, and triggers that influence their actions and decisions. Through self-reflection and mindfulness practices, individuals can deepen their awareness of themselves and their interactions with the world around them.

By honing this self-awareness, individuals create a fertile ground for personal growth and transformation. Central to the process of self-discovery is the recognition of fundamental values and beliefs. These core principles serve as guiding lights that shape one's identity, aspirations, and relationships.

By identifying and clarifying these values, individuals can align their actions and choices with what truly matters to them. This alignment fosters a sense of authenticity and integrity, allowing individuals to live in accordance with their deepest convictions.

In exploring and affirming these foundational values, individuals establish a sense of purpose and direction that propels them forward on their journey of self-discovery. Embracing vulnerability is another essential aspect of the self-discovery process. To truly understand oneself, individuals must be willing to confront their fears, insecurities, and imperfections.

By acknowledging and accepting their vulnerabilities, individuals open themselves up to self-discovery and growth. Vulnerability fosters authenticity and genuine connections with others as individuals become more open and honest about their inner experiences.

By embracing vulnerability, individuals cultivate resilience and inner strength, empowering them to navigate challenges and setbacks with grace and courage. Exploring inner desires and passions is a deeply enriching aspect of the self-discovery journey.

By delving into what truly ignites their spirit and brings them joy, individuals uncover hidden aspects of themselves that may have been overlooked or suppressed. This exploration enables individuals to connect with their authentic selves, tapping into a wellspring of creativity, purpose, and fulfillment. By indulging in activities that resonate with their passions, individuals nourish their soul and cultivate a sense of wholeness and vitality. This alignment with their innermost desires fuels a sense of purpose and meaning, infusing their lives with a profound sense of fulfillment and satisfaction.

Releasing external expectations is a pivotal step in the process of self-discovery. Often, individuals are burdened by societal norms, cultural pressures, and external judgments that influence their sense of self and worth.

By letting go of these external expectations and definitions, individuals free themselves to explore and embrace their authentic essence. This liberation from external constraints allows individuals to define success, happiness, and fulfillment on their terms, rather than conforming to external standards.

By releasing these societal constructs, individuals reclaim their autonomy and agency, allowing their true selves to emerge and flourish. Embracing change and growth is fundamental to the journey of self-discovery. As individuals delve deeper into their inner selves and unearth hidden aspects of their identity, they may encounter resistance, discomfort, or uncertainty.

Embracing these challenges as opportunities for growth and transformation allows individuals to evolve and expand beyond their current limitations. Change is a constant in life, and by embracing it with openness and resilience, individuals can navigate transitions and transformations with grace and adaptability.

By embracing the process of growth and change, individuals embark on a continual journey of self-discovery and personal evolution. The path to self-discovery is a marathon, not a sprint. It is a gradual and unfolding process that requires patience, dedication, and self-compassion. Rather than fixating on a specific outcome or destination, individuals are encouraged to embrace the journey itself and savor the insights and revelations it brings.

Each step taken towards self-discovery unveils new layers of understanding and self-awareness, enriching the individual's experience and deepening their connection to themselves.

By recognizing the inherent value of the process, individuals can cultivate a sense of gratitude and acceptance for each moment of self-discovery, fostering a profound sense of fulfillment and meaning in their lives. In conclusion, the journey of self-discovery is an inward odyssey that holds the potential to transform, inspire, and enrich individuals in profound ways.

By embarking on this path with courage, curiosity, and openness, individuals can unravel the layers of their identity, revealing the essence of their true selves. Through self-awareness, values alignment, vulnerability, passion exploration, release of external expectations, and embrace of change and growth, individuals can embark on a transformative journey of self-discovery that leads to a life of authenticity, fulfillment, and purpose.

The process of self-discovery is a lifelong pursuit, a continual unfolding of the self that promises deep insights, meaningful connections, and profound growth. Embrace the journey, trust the process, and uncover the boundless possibilities that await on the path to understanding and embracing your true essence.

May all be free from sorrow and the causes of sorrow.
May all never be separated from the sacred happiness
which is sorrowless; And may all live in equanimity,
without too much attachment and too much aversion,
And live believing in the equality of all that lives.
Om Mani Pädme Hum